JOHN ELIASBERG

COIN
COLLECTING
FOR BEGINNERS

TABLE OF CONTENTS

INTRODUCTION

People collect coins for a variety of purposes. Collectors that collect coins based on their expected future value can be found. Many people collect coins once because of the metal variety, and some for the historical worth of the coin. Others enjoy checking mint markings and dates on their daily change and enjoy collecting common coins. Others have an extensive collection of coins from other nations. From the 1800s until the early 1900s, many coin collectors spend thousands of dollars on rare gold and silver coins. Anyone of any age can enjoy and benefit from the hobby of coin collecting. Many coin collectors started collecting as children, collecting dimes or cents, and many have made coin collecting a lifelong passion. It necessitates initial financial investment; thus, joining a coin collectors' organization to acquire ideas and assistance from qualified and experienced collectors is recommended.

You'll need someone to buy your coins from, and it can be difficult to find a reputable coin dealer if you're new to the pastime. Having someone who has been doing this for a long time can be invaluable in guiding you toward a trustworthy and competent coin dealer. Begin by obtaining a large magnifying lens and inspecting coins in a bright environment to spot mintmarks, mistakes, and date reading on old or damaged coins.

To start your coin collecting journey, first select the coins you want to add to your collection and obtain a "bookshelf folder" for each one. Additionally, you will need appropriate storage solutions, such as clear plastic or screw-top coin tubes, to ensure the safety of your coins until they are ready to be placed in a coin album. It is also beneficial to have storage for duplicate coins. It's important to become familiar with the various coin values and keep track of dealer pricing, as this will help you understand which coins are sold and their corresponding prices. Finally, it is essential to have someone who can guide you in assessing the mint mark, age, color, surface, and condition of a coin accurately. Consider seeking out the assistance of one or more individuals with experience in this area.

The newspaper, particularly the section on numismatics, will be of great interest to you as you get more active and interested in your passion and want to keep up with current events in the world of numismatics.

As you gain more expertise with coin collecting, your "eye for coins" will improve and mature to the point where you'll be studying features and nuances like coin lettering more closely, ensuring sure the letters aren't blemished or blurred but still discernible. You'll be so engrossed in the coin's common state that you'll unintentionally dismiss coins that exhibit signs of abrasion, and you'll miss out on the fun of coin collecting.

Take your time to read, examine images, gain insights from other collectors, and ask as many questions as necessary to both fellow collectors and dealers. Coin collecting is a pastime that can endure as long as you do. Your expertise and abilities will help you save and earn money when the occasion arises, but most importantly, you'll enjoy the learning process.

BOOK 1 - THE BASIC OF COIN COLLECTION

CHAPTER 1

UNDERSTANDING COIN COLLECTION

The hobby of coin collecting is the oldest in the world. Coin collecting has been a popular pastime for many centuries, and Numismatics is the term for coin collecting. Numismatics and coin collecting are inextricably related. Coin collecting is one of the most enjoyable and popular pastimes. It is a different type of legal tender or coin dealing. You can collect coins for various reasons, including historical worth, the fact that some coins are excluded from a single period, the coin's future perceived value, or the metal type, among others.

The history of money is concerned with the evolution of systems that perform the functions of money throughout history. There are many ways to trade wealth through these systems, but direct bartering isn't the same. Money serves as a medium for this exchange. Money changes its forms over time. In modern times, a written or electronic account can represent money as well as coins and notes. Depending on how you look at it, it could have real value (commodity money), be legally convertible into real value or representative money, or have no real value at all, known as fiat money.

The money didn't arrive until later. From natural objects to coins to paper to digital versions, its form has changed over the years and millennia. People have been exchanging money as a means of payment, a standard of value, a repository for wealth, and an accounting unit regardless of its format for centuries. As early as 700 years, Europeans, Asians, and Africans were all connected through the Maritime Silk Road trading route. This global trade was both transformative and foundational.

A Brief History of Old Coins

Evidence has recently emerged to challenge the traditional belief that coin collecting started during the Italian Renaissance. Suetonius, a Roman historian who lived from AD 69 to 122, wrote about Augustus' love for ancient and foreign coins, which he gave as gifts to his friends. Other literary sources from the Greek and Roman periods also refer to coin collections. In addition to these accounts, archaeological findings suggest that coins have been collected since at least the Roman era. For instance, a hoard of 70 Roman gold coins discovered in Switzerland contained no two specimens of the same type, indicating that the coins were likely gathered under the administration of the Roman town. Art collecting, which is a broader discipline that includes coin collecting, is believed to have started as early as the 4th or 3rd century BC. At that time, coins were regarded as works of art, and they were among the most affordable and portable art pieces. It is no wonder that they were collected as they were valued more than their monetary worth and were often used in decorative art and jewelry of that period.

The Roman Mint created a series of coins commemorating all of the deified emperors from Augustus to Severus Alexander during the reign of Trajanus Decius (AD 249–251).

The designs on these coins were based on those issued by the revered rulers, with some of the original coins dating back nearly 300 years. The Mint needed examples of coins to use as prototypes, and such an arrangement is difficult to conceive as anything other than a collection. Charlemagne created a series of coins in AD 805 that closely match the style and subject matter of Roman Imperial issues—yet another example of collected coins serving as inspiration for die engravers in the future.

In the 12th and 13th centuries, Nestorian scholars and artisans working for the princes of the Jazira (Mesopotamia, now Iraq, Syria, and Turkey) created a superb series of coins with themes based on ancient Greek and Roman problems.

Some are so similar to the originals' details that even the inscriptions are carefully repeated.

Others were altered in unusual ways. The sole difference between the reverse of a Romanus III Byzantine coin and its Islamic counterpart, for example, is that the cross has been removed from the emperor's orb following Muslim sensibilities. The wide range of these photographs and their skillful utilization show the existence of well-researched collections. In his 1901 work Traité des monnaies Grecques et Romaines, the prominent French numismatist Ernest Babylon mentions a document from 1274 called Thesaurus Maagnus in medalis auri optimii, which records a formal collection of ancient coins at a monastery in Padua, Italy.

Petrarch (1304–1374), a famous Italian Renaissance scholar, amassed a significant scientific and artistic collection of ancient coins. In these early centuries, fascination with the artwork on the coins—depictions of historical kings, mythological characters, and the like—seems to have sparked a lot of interest in collecting.

Until recently, collecting was not common in Asia and Africa due to the lack of imagery on Asian and African coins. The establishment of an active market is the fundamental distinction between coin collecting before and after the Renaissance.

With the resurgence of interest, demand for antique coins far outstripped supply. Ancient coin collecting became the "hobby of kings" in the 15th and 16th centuries, and the list of collectors is a list of European nobility. At the same time, these patrons commissioned prominent artists to create copies of ancient coins and portrait or commemorative medals, which were collectible in and of themselves.

Collectors' appetites encouraged a cottage business of agents and a search for salable artifacts in source areas. As one could assume, the ravenous market supported the development of forgeries by creating such high demand.

The nature of gathering had slowly evolved toward severe investigation by the 17th century. As a result, extensive collections were formed, researched, and cataloged.

Numismatics became an academic subject during this time, and numerous significant treatises were published. Institutional engagement and the expansion of public collections in the 18th century led to academic study sponsorship, elevating numismatics to the status of a science. Most importantly, detailed and widely published treatises on coinage and collecting institutionalized the flow of information and new findings. During this time, many of the noble families' huge private collections fell under state authority, and the following cataloging of these holdings contributed volumes to existing knowledge. Because this information was readily available to the general public, coin collecting became a hobby among middle-class merchants and people of many professions as their numbers and cultural sophistication increased. Ancient coin collecting is one of the few ways the regular individual can own authentic antiquity artifacts, and the rising collector base recognized this. Coins are incredibly accessible historical artifacts.

In modern times:

Personal coin collectors grew substantially during the nineteenth century; also handbooks for beginners began to come out. The scope of coin collecting expanded from ancient coins to world coinage, and it became a popular leisure pursuit. Numismatic organizations sprang up all over the Europe, United Kingdom, and the United States with membership accessible to anybody. Coin collecting periodicals began to appear, and the increased interest of new enthusiasts resulted in a thriving industry.

The coin collecting union grew even more prominent by introducing coin exhibits, numismatic conventions, academic symposia, international conferences, and a profusion of local club in the twentieth century. Some of these clubs merged to establish enormous and influential organizations. At the same time, trade organizations were formed to bring the community of professional numismatists or coin dealers closer together. During this time, a thriving coin market began to emerge.

Previously, only the wealthy could afford to buy antique coins, and there were few sources. As the general public became more aware of ancient coins as collectibles and an enormous demand emerged on the market, local merchants put tremendous effort into locating sources. As a result, ancient sites were widely excavated. Farmers, who discovered coins and minor artifacts on their tilled ground regularly, came to recognize the value of these artifacts.

Hundreds of thousands of coins were found, auctioned, and distributed throughout Europe's cultural centers. This created a situation where the scarcity of specific coin kinds could be observed and assessed.

Many ancient coins were produced in large quantities, still flooding the market and resulting in highly cheap pricing. At the same time, the value of scarce coins increased. As a result, beginning coin collectors will find ancient coins quite affordable, while seasoned collectors will find choice and rare examples expensive and challenging to get.

The market's growth also led to coins advertising as an investment tool. Several investors have amassed private collections of collectible coins. In the late 1980s and early 1990s, at least two prominent funds for ancient coin investment were traded on the New York Stock Exchange. A variety of funds and outlets trade modern gold coins as bullion. Even yet, most coin collecting is done as a pastime.

The subject of forgery or counterfeit has grown severe increasingly to collectors as contemporary technology has advanced over the last two centuries. False issues have always existed.

A lot of coins were faked in ancient times, either for profit or unnecessary. The latter happened because legal money was not always on hand for circulation. It was especially prevalent in Gaul, Spain and Britain.

The term forgery differs from the term counterfeiting in that the forger aims to sell his items to collectors, regardless of their legal currency value. Collectors and forgers have waged a centuries-long battle of wits. Fortunately, the collector has access to the same tools that the forger does. The great number of forgery is discovered over time.

Collecting something is a behavior that has its roots in primal instinct. The method of collecting coins, on the other hand, can differ substantially from one collector to the economic, historical, next. Political, aesthetic, and current approaches are the most common. Some collectors, for example, want to amass a complete set of portrait of prominent persons in a small or broad topic. Others may concentrate on the metallurgical or denominational ties of particular topics. Historical events have always been a trendy theme for coin issuing authorities and collectors. Throughout history, coins have mirrored the artistic fashions of the time. As a result, they offer a diverse range of sources and an excellent collection of miniature-art to today's art students and enthusiasts. Coins offer a wide range of topics from which to prefer and build a collection. This hobby's extensive and continuing popularity can be attributed to its deep and various degrees of appeal.

For the mainly part, paper currency collection began in the nineteenth century. Scarcity boosts the object's value, as it does with any collecting, but collectors may be interested in the historical significance of note. Confederate States of America printed currency during short periods in history, such as the Russian occupation notes that circulated in Soviet-controlled territories during and after World War II, are examples of short-lived currency. During World War II, Nazi prisoners in camps like Theresienstaadt printed and used currency unique to the time and location of the camp.

The Internet ushered in a whole new generation of numismatic enthusiasts. More new collectors were born due to extensive exposure to a stunningly big audience than the leisure pursuit had seen in years. This presented new opportunities as well as new obstacles. Because Internet buyers had limited experience, false marketplaces were formed that could not be sustained in a long run. The Internet market gradually settled down after a surge of interest in the mid-1990s, becoming a platform where deep-rooted enterprises could deal with better effect than in other usual venues. The development of learning sites simultaneously allowed new collectors to mature at a much speedy rate.

Controlling the integrity of vendors who emerge anonymously from the expanse of cyberspace has been one of the most challenging difficulties for Internet shopping sites. Coin collecting became more fashionable, and coin collectors gave historical coins protection. In 1970, an organization UNESCO enacted a resolution designating coins and further artifacts older than hundred years as cultural assets and recommending restrictions on their export, import, and transferring of ownership. Every member state that voted in favor of resolution was permitted to design its enforcement mechanism. As an outcome, several ancient coin-producing countries now forbid the export of antique coins. The law that gears the UNESCO declaration in the United States allows for restrictions in specific circumstances.

Museums and Private collectors often oppose import limitations. Nationalist regimes and archaeological advocacy groups are the leading proponents of such control. Collectors groups see the British Treasure Act and Portable Antiquities Scheme (BTAP) both implemented in the mid-1990s era as a feasible mechanism for preserving cultural assets and protecting individual liberties.

1.1 WHAT IS WORTH COLLECTING?

It's entirely up to you what to collect. It will always be a category that piques the collector's attention while remaining within their financial constraints. Historic coins, world coins (coins from several countries), and coins of a certain country are some of the most popular types of collections. It is often beneficial to specialize within these classifications. When collecting from a specific country, you can deal with many series, commemoratives, a typeset, die variants, errors, paper currency, and so on. Set limits on the coin grades you collect, such as all VF, G-VG, better, or uncirculated. You may go after the entire series. For a series collector, the ultimate goal is to acquire every mintmark and date, including notable variations in design. As an example, the United States Standing Liberty quarter was produced in Philadelphia, San Francisco, and Denver from 1916 to 1930. However, coins were not minted at all three facilities each year, and there were no coins minted at either location in 1922. Furthermore, the obverse underwent significant changes in 1917, and a complete set is typically considered to consist of both designs from each mint for that year.

When building a type collection, a collector aspires to have one of each series and significant design variety within each series. Coinage from the

United States or Canada in the twentieth century are examples. You could choose to focus on old coins. This refers to coins struck before the year 500. Many of them stick to a theme, which is one way to keep your collection focused. According to experts, ancient copper, gold, and silver coins are still easily available and less expensive than you might think.

Collectors of tokens are a popular group as they are fascinated by the history behind these small, unique pieces. In times when there were not enough low-value coins being produced, traders and merchants had to take things into their own hands and create tokens. This practice dates back to mid-1600s in England and continued into the 1790s and 1810s. These tokens served as a regional currency and were outlawed several times by Parliament, although they continued to be sold and used well into the mid-nineteenth century, often under the guise of "advertising tickets." Tokens were roughly the same size as farthings, which were also in short supply at the time. By the end of Queen Victoria's reign, the need for tokens had diminished, but similar items, such as checks distributed at bars, were still in use. These were so common that no one bothered to track how they were used.

Cooperative societies used checks to record the valuation of completed transactions to ensure that the right dividend amount could be paid. Depending on the amount of fruit gathered, fruit pickers were given tally sheets. Vending machines, gaming, and public transit are the most modern uses of tokens. Even though they are less valuable than coins, tokens are far more interesting if you research regional history.

Collecting proof sets is an option worth considering. Proof coins are manufactured to sell at a premium to collectors and for exhibition or presentation as a prize or gift. Mirror-like fields, frozen designs, particularly in recent years, and other tiny characteristics distinguish proofs from normal coins.

Each proof coin die is fine-tuned to provide an extraordinarily smooth surface and is only used for a few coins to achieve these attributes. Planchets are fed into the coin press by hand and stuck at a higher pressure than usual.

With tongs or gloves, struck coins are physically retrieved. Modern proof coins are usually stored in clear plastic to protect them from handling, dampness, and other factors. The US Mint has been offering annual proof coin sets for many years. A single proof coin of each issued denomination is usually included in these "standard" proof sets. Prestige Sets were also available in 1983, 1984, and 1986-1997.

All of the coins in the regular set, plus several commemorative coins minted the same year, make up the Prestige Set. The Mint has also offered Silver Proof Sets since 1992, which include 90 percent half dollars, silver proof quarters, and dimes.

A Premier Silver Proof Set was also available from 1992 to 1998 at the Mint. The two silver proof sets include similar coins, with the premier set being wrapped more attractively. Additionally, slabs can be collected. A licensed slab or coin has been verified, graded, and framed by an expert accrediting service in a sonically sealed, durable plastic holder. The holder protects against water damage or deterioration, but it is not airtight; thus, it will not prevent toning. Because tampering with the holder will be obvious, it also prohibits the licensed coin from substituting something else.

Fake and changed coins that major certification services have slabbed are not uncommon but rare. The slabber who slabbed the coin could guarantee its authenticity. As a result, a coin slabbed by a reputable accrediting firm offers some security, particularly when counterfeits exist and the potential purchaser cannot reliably assess its genuineness. Grading is a matter of opinion, as we'll discuss later. When delivered to several services and even when "cracked out" and submitted to the same service again, the same coin may receive different grades. Furthermore, since the first slabs were manufactured in 1986, grading rules for certain uncirculated coins have changed. If a coin in an early slab is resubmitted today, it may receive different grades.

The grade on a slab represents the opinions of a few people who examined the coin when it was presented. As a result, market values for slabbed coins of equivalent grades may differ. Purchase the coin rather than the holder if at all possible. Prices range from $10 to $175.00 per coin, plus delivery fees in both ways, depending on the service and turnaround time.

The skills and techniques needed to encapsulate coins in slab-like containers could be learned faster than the knowledge needed to authenticate and grade coins correctly. The services holders are not the only ones who appear on the market. However, competent numismatists may not consider slabs from such "services" to be genuine, and they may not even be supported by a guarantee of the coin's authenticity. Knowing the service's track record and getting multiple opinions on a coin's condition can help you avoid overpaying for it.

Some coin collectors are particularly interested in international coinage. This is the name given to collections of modern coins worldwide. Geographical curiosity is common among world currency collectors. Through their collecting, they can "travel the world" in a sense.

Getting representative examples from each nation or issuing authority is a popular way to collect world coins. Some people collect by topic, such as discovering animal-themed coins from worldwide. Because global coins are usually inexpensive, this could be a good place for kids to start. Many children find foreign money by looking beneath change-to-cash machines, where customers dump coins found in penny jars. Some of these may be from South Africa, Canada, or Mexico.

Here are a few more ideas for organizing your coin collection and focusing your efforts.

Compile a collection of coins from a single country or a group of countries. A kind or series collector aims to acquire each type or series of coins, such as Lincoln pennies or US eagles. You could choose to concentrate on coins made of a certain metal, such as silver or gold. Consider collecting coins with a special design, such as animal-themed coins, boat-themed coins, or various commemorative coins, such as Olympic medals.

Some collectors are particularly interested in coins that have flaws in the pattern, structure, date, or engraving. Non-monetary coin collections, such as commemorative tokens and battle medals, are another area of expertise. Save a quarter, dime, penny, and nickel from the year you were born. Look through each Mint for one. The Philadelphia Mint and the Denver Mint in Colorado produce different coins. Make a collection of coins representing each year since your birth. They're in both mints, so keep an eye out. Coins from worldwide can be found on a map, locate their countries. Learn about the meanings of the images on the coins for the country.

1.2 Why Collect Coins?

The pastime of coin collecting provides numerous advantages that you may not have considered previously. You've come to the right location if you have a hunger for information. Finding coins and putting them in a folder or box isn't the only part of collecting. Coins carry a lot of information about the time they were created and historical individuals. If you come across a particularly intriguing coin, the Royal Mint website (www.royalmint.com) is an excellent place to go to learn more about it. Now we can see some significant and valuable steps:

- Coin collecting is a hobby that teaches and informs you about the background, culture, history, politics, and so on. A dedicated coin collector should endeavor to learn and understand the history of the coins.

- If coin collecting is a hobby for you, you can join several libraries and subscribe to coin world and numismatic news. Always try to figure out what kind of coin you're collecting.

- It teaches you how to be patient and achieve a positive outcome.

- Collecting many coins in a short period is difficult or impossible. You will have to wait for a long day to discover the perfect mate, so be patient throughout this time.

- It aids in the formation of positive interpersonal relationships. A good friendship will assist you in achieving your objective.

- It teaches you how to grade coins and provides you with information.

- A coin collection is one type of investment. Although it is a short-term investment, you must consider the long-term implications. As a result, it teaches you how to keep your coins and make long-term plans properly.

- The coin collecting hobby always strives to remind or encourage you to focus on quality rather than quantity.

Everyone does it for their reasons. Whether or not it was a secret pastime, the ancient kings did it for the sake of their position of power. You have a unique reason for collecting coins, unlike any other coin enthusiast. Some people do it by accident because they are fascinated by coins, particularly those dating back several generations.

Isn't it cool to own a coin from the 1700s, before you even existed?

As for me, I'd think it was like stepping back in time to the days of Abraham Lincoln. Inadvertent coin collectors may never amass sufficient coins to assemble a collection. These people are intent on pursuing this practice. Your motivation and direction will be guided by it.

The following are some of the more popular justifications for coin collecting:

In which category are you?

As A Real Investment:

Coins have a monetary value to some collectors. Money made from precious metals can fetch millions of dollars, as extremely rare coins. These coin specialists are looking for high-grade, scarce, and in-demand coins that will fetch a premium on the secondary market.

If so, what's your primary goal?

To learn about the value of coins, the materials they are made of, and which ones are in demand, you will have to do a lot of research. To make smart acquisition decisions, you should remember that you may have to buy most of these valuable coins.

It's critical to realize that you may not see a return on your investment for several years or even a decade from now. Make sure you're ready to put in the time if you decide to participate. In the long run, your investments will pay off if you make smart acquisitions now.

Throughout his long career, John J. Pittman Jr. amassed a world-class collection as a coin collector and numismatist. It was a challenge to find rare and high in value coins, but he did his best.

The coin collection of David W. Akers sold for $30 million in 1997. An 1883 Capped Head gold five-dollar half eagle coin, purchased for $635 in 1954, was part of this collection. It was sold for $467,500 in 1997, an increase in value! Just think about it. All because of one valuable asset that John used when collecting coins, namely knowledge. You must be familiar with your currency.

To Learn Something About History:

Some people collect them as a way to preserve the past. Rather than the copper used today, imagine holding a 1943 US penny or an ancient coin featuring a portrait of an earlier century leader like Alexander the Great. Carrying around relics from the past is a fun experience. It is a reminder of how far we have come, as well as evidence of the existence of generations before us. In other words, it transports you back to a time before you even existed. Being a historical coin collector is an exciting and rewarding endeavor. In this case, there's no mention of value. A great deal of attention is paid to the date, year, and any notable events during that time and the portrait of the person depicted on the coin. Investigate the history of each coin to record and label it on the coin case – or wherever you want to put it.

As A Hobby:

Putting together a collection is a big draw for some people. Whether they're eager to find a particular coin or complete a set of coins, their motivations vary. It could be as simple as appreciating the artistic value of the coins. If you're collecting coins just for fun, it doesn't matter what coins you order as long as they're neatly organized. A piggy bank full of coins does not constitute a collection.

Classifying and organizing your coins so that you can easily identify each one is an important part of keeping track of your collection's history and origins. To give just a few examples, there could be a section devoted to old coins from the 18th century, new coins from the 20th century, and so on. Apart from that, gather whatever gives you a rush or rushes you.

To Pass On To The Next Generation As A Legacy:

Having a coin collection can be a wonderful legacy to leave your children. After your death, it could serve as a lasting reminder of who you were. If we could face the facts, paper and coin money may not exist in the future. The general population is already accepting Bitcoin and other forms of intangible currency.

It is not clear will ever be used for business transactions, but who knows?

What is the value of a coin collection as a physical representation of money?

It'll be a priceless possession to have. As the value of coins rises over time and their rarity is taken into account, your collection will be a gold mine. Your future generations could greatly benefit from your investment or hobby right now. There are various reasons why coin collecting is a popular pastime, from a financial standpoint to documenting the past. Finding and obtaining those coins will be a life-changing experience for you. The more coins you amass, the more proud you should be of yourself. It's both exciting and rewarding.

1.3 Kinds of Coins

You've previously studied the many components of a coin, along with some of the fundamental phrases that all coin collectors should be familiar with. Now is the time to delve a little further and learn about the many types of coins and their differences. Coins can be classified based on various factors, such as the material used to make them or the occasion they were struck. To make things easier for you, we won't go into too much detail about the specific categories instead of presenting you with the most common coin types in general.

Coins of Gold and Silver:

Most countries have used silver and gold as their currency since ancient times. Ancient Greece, Rome, Egypt, and even England and the United States are examples of this. Gold and silver coins are no longer used in regular transactions, but collectors highly seek them. Depending on what type of gold or silver coin you're looking for, the cost of such a piece can be rather high.

Commemorative Coins:

Commemorative coins became popular in the United States in the 1930s when the US Mint was obligated to produce them. They were sold to distributors, who tacked a premium to the coin's face value. This, however, did not last long, as collectors began to complain about speculators manipulating the market and pricing. As a result, the United States Mint created fewer commemorative coins. The first wave of commemorative coins drew many individuals into coin collecting, and they continue to do so today. Commemorative coins are appealing and elegant to coin collectors and people interested in coin collecting in general.

REVOLUTIONARY COINS:

In a nutshell, revolutionary coins were issued during periods of revolution, such as the American Revolution of 1776. These coins can be fairly valuable depending on other criteria due to their historical significance.

ANCIENT COINS:

Ancient coins are frequently confused with gold and silver coinage. In ancient periods, coins were made from different materials such as ivory, glass, or porcelain. Another common misunderstanding regarding ancient coins is that they are prohibitively pricey. While this may be true in some cases, you can still own one or more without breaking the bank because a coin's market value is not only influenced by its age.

PENNIES AS SOUVENIRS:

These coins have a lot of potentials. They're regular coins that have been pressed, stretched, and altered somehow. The most intriguing detail about them is that mutilating coins to put them back into circulation is banned except for these souvenir pennies. This is a fun addition to any collector's collection!

MEDALLIONS:

The term "medallion" is often used to denote a wide range of coins (including commemorative coins). In general, "medallions" refer to any round, ornamented piece of metal with some importance associated with it (such as monetary value, for example). On the other hand, actual medallions are rarely accompanied by legal tender.

TOKENS:

Trade tokens are extremely rare and valuable collectibles. They can be worth hundreds of dollars in some cases, for example, Civil War tokens. Typically, tokens were made during financial hardship when silver and gold were rare, but people still required a form of payment. Tokens were often for $1 or less at face value, although some tokens can be worth as much as $5 and utilized in ordinary transactions like "standard" circulation coins.

ERROR COINS:

These coins had an error a double denomination, an over date, or a brokerage. The errors came out of the Mint in this condition, and some may be persuaded to believe they are worthless. On the other hand, error coins can be fairly expensive depending on the flaw and the era they came from.

BU ROLLS:

BU Rolls are emblematic of the new generation of coin collectors that emerged at the end of the 1950s and 1960s. These "rolls" were bank-wrapped Brilliant Uncirculated little stashes of coins that drove collectors insane throughout the time.

Collectors learned that, although some of these BU rolls were represented as rare, they were relatively common, and their 15-minute glory began to wane (as the millions had manufactured them). As a result, BU Rolls are often startlingly low in price these days, so you may want to avoid falling into a trap with them.

SILVER CERTIFICATES:

People utilized old Silver Certificates to exchange one silver dollar. These certificates, however, were only valid until 1964, when the government stopped producing them. For a time, however, people could exchange their silver certificates for a specific amount of silver, which sparked a whole new craze in the coin collecting world as everyone "suddenly" began seeking these. Like earlier fads, this one drew many people into the realm of coin collecting.

ART BARS:

Art bars were rather popular in the 1970s, which was a bit of an oddity. They were one-ounce thin rectangular silver bars with polished surfaces and designs commemorating pretty about anything you could think of, from your wedding to your kitten. Art bars were highly sought after because mintages were initially limited. However, the market became saturated with these art bars, and customers finally became tired of them. Like the other coins on our list that sparked a new trend, art bars drew many collectors into the world of coins. There is no such thing as a "proper" or "wrong" coin to collect. Sure, some coins have more worth now than others, but at the end of the day, the value is determined by many things, not just the type of coin.

1.4 Themes for Coin Collection

Aside from the Roosevelt Dime, various coin collecting options you can start. This is part of what makes coin collecting so exciting and distinctive, with millions of achievable combinations and subjects to choose from. Here are some suggestions for new collectors:

Year Collections:

Collecting coins by year is the most popular coin collecting theme. This can be accomplished in several ways. For example, you could collect every coin for a single country for a specified year, such as your birthday or the first time man walked on the moon in 1969. Alternatively, you might gather all years of a single coin kind, such as all from 1946 Roosevelt Dimes to the present.

Time Period Coins:

History fans will enjoy this method of collecting coins from a particular time with historical relevance. If you're interested in World War I, then you can collect every U.S. and country coin from 1914 to 1918. Or during Abraham Lincoln's presidency, which lasted from 1860 to 1865.

Country Collections:

The country where you live is another popular theme. You can also strive to acquire a diverse range of coins worldwide. This is the big hit with the younger ones. Holding the same coin and year with different mint marks is also a typical technique to put together a collection, usually an extension of collecting by year.

Series and Typeset:

A series collects coins for a specific period, like all Roosevelt Dimes. You'd have to gather not only the mintmarks but also the years. A type set is a collection of coins that includes each significant design for a specific denomination, for example the Liberty Head Nickel, Jefferson Nickel, Shield Nickel, and Buffalo Nickel.

ERROR COINS:

A new frequent idea is concentrating on mistake coins for a specific type, denomination. Typical mistake coins include general strikes, off-center, and strikes multiple strikes,

WORLD COINS:

Overseas coins are interesting to collect coins, outside of the United States. Foreign and world coins can be collected in various ways, including in multiple languages, coins with holes, bi-metallic coins etc.

ANCIENT COINS:

These are coins those are thousands of years old. Another unusual way to acquire a portion of history is to collect ancient coins. Coins have to be manufactured individually or by hand before being struck by technology. Ancient coin collectors are particularly fond of Roman and Greek coins.

COIN COMPOSITION:

Some people choose to concentrate on the composition or metals of the coins. Collectors of silver, gold, copper and platinum are all famous metals. Silver coins, especially silver dollars, are a favorite of many collectors.

CHAPTER 2

THE ANATOMY OF A COIN

The coin depicted is called 1952 Franklin Half Dollar. When speaking with other collectors or dealers, knowing the terminologies for coin anatomy is essential. The motto, date, mintmark, designer's initials, and denomination are all located in different places on each piece. Study the language and be well-versed in it.

DATE: The year the coin was minted or manufactured is indicated by the date.

DENOMINATION: Represents the coin's monetary worth.

DESIGNER'S INITIALS: The designer's initials may be found on almost every coin, and you may have to look for them; they are 'JRS' for John R. Sinnock on this coin.

EDGE: The edge of the coin, which can be plain (smooth), adorned, or reeded.

FIELD: The unused and flat area of the coin acts as a background.

LEGEND: The major lettering of the coin or inscription is called the legend. The country from which the currency originated is usually stated.

MINT MARK: The letter or symbol on the coin that denotes where it was manufactured or struck is known as the mintmark. Single letters are used to locate cities in the United States, and the 'D' on the coin above stands for Denver, Colorado. On US coins, you'll find the following:

Philadelphia, Pennsylvania (abbreviated as P or blank) is a city in the United States.

Mint of Denver Mark

D – Denver, Colorado W – West Point, New York

S is the abbreviation for San Francisco, California.

Charlotte, North Carolina (C) is a city in the United States.

D – Dahlonega, Georgia (1838–1861) CC – Carson City, Nevada

New Orleans, Louisiana (O)

MOTTO: 'E Pluribus Unum' and 'In God, We Trust' are the mottos on most US coins. Older US coins have a different design.

OBSERVE/HEAD: The front side of the coin, sometimes known as the "obverse" or the "head."

PORTRAIT: The portrait on the coin's obverse side is probably its most distinguishing feature. In most cases, a US President or historical figure and Lady Liberty are shown.

RELIEF: Any raised coin feature other than the field is a relief.

REVERSE/TAIL: The backside of the coin, often known as the "tail" or "reverse."

RIM: The slightly raised outer edge of the coin makes it easier to stack and protect the coin's face.

SCAN THE FOLLOW QR CODE TO RECEIVE

THE 10 EXTREMELY USEFUL TIPS FOR BUYING
RARE COINS ONLINE

CHAPTER 3

NUMISMATIC LANGUAGE

Coin collectors speak a unique language and use specific terms when discussing coin collecting like any other community or social group. Do you want to spend time with other numismatists and have no idea what they say when talking about this fascinating subject? To make matters worse, approaching a coin dealer and insisting on explaining every term isn't a pleasant experience. If you don't speak the language, you're at risk of being taken advantage of because it's easy to be fooled if you don't know your way around coins.

Numismatics is generally defined as the systematic acquisition and study of coins. As a result, coin collecting has become a subset of numismatics. Numismatics encompasses a wide range of money-related items, including coins, tokens, currency, checks, medals, stock certificates, and other items that represent current and past financial assets or liabilities. Numismatists include those who study the field of numismatics and coin collectors.

Although no one will ever tell you this, picking up the lingo is the best way to blend in and get the hang of any new practice. "Language even more than color defines who you are to people," wrote Trevor Noah in his book 'Born a crime' He was able to get by with the help of language during a time when people of his skin tone were subjected to racial profiling. The ability to speak the language of a specific social group gives you a significant advantage in the workplace. As a result, you'll need to brush up on your knowledge of coin collecting jargon. You'll be able to converse with dealers, fellow numismatists, and other coin collectors more easily. Numismatic terms and their definitions are listed below.

3.1 Terms Related To the Condition of a Coin

About Good (A.G.): It's not great, but it's also not terrible to say that a coin is "about good" because the grade of the coins is just below good. Only the most important characteristics are likely to be discernible on an A.G. coin.

Features like the mintmark, the date, and so forth are included. Some other features like portraits may also have faded away.

Abrasions: If someone says, "This coin has abrasions," or in other words, the coin has been abraded by another coin, a foreign object, or some substance (like acid).

Alternate surfaces: A coin with an altered surface is referred to, that its value has been diminished due to factors such as cleaning or polishing, making it unattractive to collectors.

Uncirculated: A coin is considered "uncirculated" if it hasn't been used in a day-to-day transaction.

ALMOST UNCIRCULATED: This coin appears to be brand new to the naked eye or at first glance as if it has never been circulated. A magnifying glass can reveal minor friction or rubs if examined closely.

NO GRADE: A coin that returns from a third-party grading service and is not encapsulated is referred to as having "no grade." Authenticity or damage could be to blame.

ARTIFICIAL TONING: To add color by using chemicals or heat on the coin's surface is a form of artificial toning.

BAG TONING: A coin can acquire some color when stored in a cloth bag containing sulfur and other metal-reactive chemicals, such as those found in sulphuric acid. Morgan silver dollars tend to develop bag toning.

BROWN: The term "brown" refers to a copper coin that has lost its red color due to various factors. The word "brown" can be abbreviated as B.N. when describing a coin in grading.

ALTERATION refers to a coin with its mintmark or date altered to make it appear to be a rare or valuable issue.

A CARBON SPOT: Discoloration on the surface of a coin is known as a "carbon spot." A planchet imperfection before the coin's striking and improper storage is possible causes. Carbon spots are nearly impossible to remove without leaving pits on the surface, no matter the reason. Carbon spots diminish the value and quality of a coin.

BASAL STATE: A coin is said to be in this state if it's in a condition consistent with its basic form, which means that it can only be identified by the mintmark, date, and type of the coin. One-year coins may not have a visible date on them.

A CLEANED COIN: When cleaned with mild abrasives, it can be restored to its original condition. It will likely lose its natural color and luster and appear washed out if treated with baking soda. A coin that has been "cleaned" is referred to as such.

QUESTIONABLE TONING: The term refers to the suspicion that a coin's color is artificial, not natural.

RAW: Ungraded coins are known as "raw" in this context.

SEMI-COMMONS: Coins classified as semi-common fall in the middle of the rarity and commonness spectrum.

ULTRA-RARE: Coins or numismatic artifacts that are extremely rare are included in this category. Only a few examples/pieces of evidence are needed.

3.2 TERM USED TO DESCRIBE CHARACTERISTICS

BUST: In a coin's bust design, the head, neck, and upper shoulders are all included.

DENOMINATION: The face value of each coin is referred to as "denomination." When you inquire about a coin's "denomination," you're referring to its actual weight.

FACE VALUES: A coin's "face value" refers to its legal issue. One pound, one dollar, or fifty pence is the unit of measure.

COIN ATTRIBUTES: the parts of a coin that make up its design, grade, luster, strike, and marks; these are the primary characteristics and the ability to catch the eye.

MINTMARK: Coins are identified by the mintmark, a small letter that appears on the coin's surface or the place where it was struck, the mint.

RELIEF: An area of a coin's design, known as a relief, is raised above the rest of the coin's surface.

THE INCUSE: This refers to the coin's legal issue. So, for example, is one dollar, one pound, or 50 pence.

LEGAL TENDER: a form of money recognized by the government: A type of currency issued and exchanged for financial transactions.

BI-METALLIC: This coin is bi-metallic, which means it is made of two different metals at once.

CIRCULATION: It means how much a coin has worth in the real world. Coins that have been used in transactions are also referred to as "spent coins."

BULLION COINS: This is a one-of-a-kind coin made of a precious metal such as gold. This is an extremely valuable coin.

ARROWS: On most U.S. coins, you'll see this design element in the left claw of the eagle.

OBSERVE: Known as "heads," a front side of a coin

REVERSE: Known as "tails," a backside of a coin.

TERMS RELATED TO MINT PLACE:

C: This mint mark identifies where a coin was struck at the Charlotte, NC mint.

CC: A mintmark refers to a coin struck at the Carson City, Nevada branch.

S-MINT: San Francisco mint coins are referred to as S-minted coins.

CLASSIC ERA: Coins from the classic era were produced between 1792 and 1964, during which time silver and gold coins were in circulation of the United States were made available for public use; they were meant to be spent in commerce. The 'classic era' refers to this time.

LISTER: When discussing coins, the term "luster" refers to the coin's ability to reflect light. It's a tool for grading coins. However, luster should be used with caution when grading a coin because it can be difficult to tell if it is artificial or natural, depending on how it was made. The luster of a surface can be reduced by cleaning, wear, and friction.

3.3 TERMS OF DENOMINATIONS

PENNY: Another name for a one-cent coin in the United States is a "penny."

NICKEL: Five-cent U.S. coins are commonly referred to as nickels.

DIME: A dime is one-tenth of a U.S. dollar (10 cents).

SOME OTHER TERMS:

PEDIGREE: The most valuable coins, such as rare bullion coins, have a higher pedigree. A coin's pedigree is a list of the current owner's information and every one of its predecessors.

SET: When you have a collection of something, you can say you have a set from a specific batch of coins. As an illustration, think of a group of half-dollars from a particular mint.

BOOK 2 – THE COIN VALUE

CHAPTER 1

THE MINT MARKS
& MINT PROCEDURE

1. MINT MARKS:

If you're new to coin collecting, learning how coins are manufactured will help you grasp the various types of coins available. It will explain why some coins are uncirculated while others are referred to as resistant coins.

ROMAN EMPIRE COIN:

Numismatics, often known as coin collecting, is derived from the Greek term "nomisma," meaning legal cash or coin. Unlike now, when we use checks, paper bills, and, increasingly, credit cards, ancient societies used coins for everyday expenditures.

COMMON COINS OF THE ROMAN EMPIRE

A free infographic by *Dirty Old Coins, LLC*

Lydia in Asia Minor, which is now part of Turkey but was under Greek influence at the time, is where the first coins were known to have been produced. They've been around for almost 2,600 years, and gold and silver alloy was used to make the first coins. The Lydian's were business-minded at the time, and they were able to create a prosperous civilization that advanced trade and commerce. Coins from this era demonstrate the evolution of coin design over time.

Pieces of gold and silver ingots were the most prevalent form of payment during the period. Because there were no standards and many dishonest merchants, each transaction involving gold and silver payment necessitated an accurate weighing of the medium.

Coins were first created around 650 B.C. and were manufactured using regulated gold and silver weights. It was marked with a government guarantee of value. The development of coinage as a primary medium of exchange occurred in the following century. Coin collection is considered to have started as soon as the first coin was produced. Because banks did not exist at the time, collecting them felt like a viable option for storing them. They were being hoarded not merely because of their intrinsic worth but also their scarcity. These coins have become a family heirloom, passed down from generation to generation. According to some experts, serious coin collecting began in the late middle Ages. Many European kings embarked on a mission to locate and collect unique coins used as currency by ancient nations. One fascinating feature they discovered was that no two coins were similar due to the procedures used to strike the coins. Coins were struck by hand, and it wasn't until the 1500s that machines began to strike coins. This activity is known as the "Hobby of Kings" because it began with these:-

EUROPEAN KINGS COINS:

During the Renaissance, coin collecting became popular, and many ambitious people made many high-quality counterfeits.

Because of its quality, antiquity, and historical relevance, even forgeries have a great value today.

I. ANCIENT COINS

WIDOW'S MITE COINS:

Artisans controlled everything from domestic goods to agricultural tools in ancient times. Making coins was one of their responsibilities. They employed minimal instruments, and the outcome was mostly dependent on their abilities. The quality of the struck coins varies, from Palestine's "widow's mite" to Greek Sicily's exquisite silver pieces. An oven for heating blanks or "flans," tongs, an anvil situated on a table or bench, and a pair of dies for impressing the design into the flan was the primary instruments used by the artisans.

Dies were made of hard bronze or iron. Bronze corroded more quickly than silver, although it was easier to engrave and not tarnish. The Greeks employed iron dies for their largest coins, which show indications of rust. The obverse die was put on the anvil, and the reverse die was struck to form the impression.

2. MODERN U.S. COINS:

In the United States, modern-era coins began in the private sector. Some coinage blanks, planchets, and other materials purchased by the U.S. Mint were made by private enterprises. In 1792, the U.S. Congress passed the Coinage Act, which established the United States Mint as part of the U.S. Treasury Department. Many foreign and colonial currencies were used before it. The new law mandated the establishment of a national mint in Philadelphia, the nation's capital at the time.

The U.S. Mint is in charge of creating, selling, and safeguarding the country's coins and assets. Between 14 and 28 billion circulation coins are produced annually, and 65 to 80 million coins are minted every day as of 2004. Only coins produced by the United States Mint are accepted as legal money in the United States. All materials needed to make U.S. coins are purchased from commercial suppliers. The U.S. Mint receives one-cent coin blanks already created, but the five-cent coin blanks and cupronickel clad coins are made from the strip.

The production procedure is essentially the same for all denominations. Dimes, quarters, half dollars, and dollars, on the other hand, go through a process known as "reeding," which leaves microscopic ridges on the coins. These ridges prevent the precious metal in gold and silver coins from being illegally shaved or clipped. It may not be as important today, but it is being done to honor a long-standing tradition of colonial times. It's also to aid visually impaired people in recognizing the coins.

All circulating coins must bear the inscriptions "Liberty," "In God We Trust," the United States of America," and "E Pluribus Unum," as well as the denomination and year of issuance as required by law. Since 1909, the slogan "In God We Trust" has been on the one-cent currency, and since 1916, on the ten-cent denomination. All half-dollar coins, gold and silver dollar coins, and quarter coins featured this inscription on July 1, 1908.

3. The Mint Procedure:

Coins are made of metal. From the preparation of the raw metals through the actual striking of the coins, various complex stages are required to manufacture them. The steps in the coin minting process are summarized here:

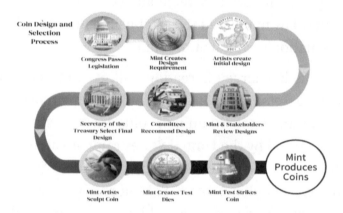

Step I: Blanking

To make the nickel, dime, quarter, half-dollar, and the dollar, the United States Mint purchases strips of a metal 13 inches broad and 1,600 feet long. The strips came in a form of coil form. Every coil is passed into a blanking-press, which punched out blanks, which are spherical discs. Webbing, the left-over strip, is sliced and recycled. After supplying manufacturers with copper and zinc, the Mint purchases ready-made cent blanks for stamping.

Blanks are planchets that have not undergone the required processing processes before being struck into coins. A planchet is a blank that has completed all required procedures and is ready to be struck. These blanks are often larger than completed coins and feature burrs on the edges, which are eliminated during the subsequent operations.

Step II: Annealing, Washing & Drying

To soften the blanks, they are heated in an annealing kiln or furnace. After that, they're put through a washing machine and dryer. The blanks harden as a result of the finish rolling and blanking activities. They're cooked to around 1400 degrees Fahrenheit in a controlled environment. The annealing procedure relaxes their crystal structure, making them easier to work with. The life of the coining dies extended due to the lower striking pressure. On the blanks, the annealing process generates minor discoloration. The blanks are thrown against one other and sent through a chemical bath to remove them.

The blanks are then dried with pressurized hot air, and if necessary, part of them are transferred to the upsetting mill.

Step III: Ridding

The blanks are screened on "riddles" before being upset to remove the wrong size or form.

Step IV: Upsetting

The good-blanks are then run throughout an upsetting mill, and a rim forms around their boundaries or edges due to this. The upsetting mill is constructed composed of a revolving wheel with a groove on one edge that fits into a curved piece with the same groove. The raised rim created throughout the operation sizes and molds the blank for improved press feed and hardens the edge to prevent metal from escaping between the obverse die and the collar.

STEP V: STRIKING

The blanks are then sent to the coining-press. They are then stamped with design and inscriptions that identify authentic U.S. coins.

STEP VI: INSPECTING

Every batch of recently struck-coins is spot-checked by press operators using magnifying lenses.

STEP VII: BAGGING AND COUNTING

Finally, the coins are counted and deposited into huge bags using an automatic counting system. The bags are preserved or sealed, placed onto the pallets and transported to vaults for the storage. Trucks deliver new coinage to Federal Reserve Banks, and the coins are then delivered to the local banks.

4. DISTRIBUTION OF COINS:

The United States Mint is constantly improving its methods for estimating coinage demand. This is to ensure that the movement of U.S. coinage is efficient and steady. The U.S. Mint plans production and coin distribution schedules using economic factors and historical seasonal trends. It's also used to calculate data related to coin production and distribution. Because forecasting isn't always correct, production must account for potential deviations. The coins are usually transported in armored tractor-trailer trucks.

CHAPTER 2

COIN GRADING AND ITS FACE VALUE

2.1 WHAT MAKES A COIN VALUABLE?

Let's take a look at two additional crucial elements before we get into what makes coins desirable to collectors:

- •The most important features of a coin, i.e., what a collector would look for.

- •The various types of coin collectors may have varying interest levels in various types of coins.

After that, analyze the primary characteristics that make coins valuable in general, as well as some examples of coveted coins you might want to look into if you're just getting started.

OTHER CHARACTERISTICS OF A COIN:

Depending on your collecting style, you may wish to consider one or more of the following coin features when deciding whether or not to purchase them:

- The term "denomination" refers to assigning Different denominations issued by each currency, for example, the penny, nickel, dime, and quarter. If you want to go all out, you might start collecting defunct denominations as well (such as the 20-cent coin, for example).

- Choose a kind of collection. This does not always pertain to the coins discussed in the last portion of our book but rather to the designs accessible for each value. A half-dollar, for example, may feature a Flowing Hair, a Franklin head, a Seated Liberty, a Walking Liberty, and so on.

- It's completely normal for some people to collect coins according to the date they were issued. For example, you might want to collect all varieties of nickels issued from 1900 to the present while skipping the extremely uncommon and expensive ones if that's what you desire.

- Combination of date and mintmark. You might also choose to organize your collection by date and mintmark. Keep in mind that this can be more expensive than simply collecting them according to their era, as most coin series feature a very valuable mintmark. This isn't true for all coins, as defined in the second bullet point of this list. Collecting all of the Barber dimes, for example, may become prohibitively expensive rare ones can cost up to $1,000,000. Collecting all of the Barber half-dollar coins, on the other hand, might be feasible.

- This type of collection contains all coins released during your birth year. If you are under 50, you can easily accomplish this by purchasing Mint sets. You might, however, choose a different goal (such as collecting all coins released in a year that is significant to you or history in general).

Now, understand that all of this may seem confusing if you are just getting started with your coin collecting, but don't worry; if you are inquisitive and study as much as you can on the subject, you will learn everything there is to know about this lucrative pastime.

5.2 COIN GRADING

WHAT IS THE BEST WAY TO GRADE YOUR COINS?

The term "grade" is used by coin experts or numismatists to describe a coin's appearance. When one coin collector informs others that he owns an uncirculated Charlotte 50 half-eagle, the other is likely to believe him. Assuming both collectors are aware of the coin's grade, they should already have an idea of its appearance.

There are arguments that grading coins for classification is more of an art than a science as it can be subjective and biased, particularly when evaluating "Mint State" coins where small differences in grade can significantly affect the price. However, grading can be learned, researched, and applied with reliable and acknowledged results based on assessment instead of personal feelings. As with any language, sport, science, or research, the most effective way to master and comprehend coin grading is to focus on learning and practicing one aspect at a time. Today, many numismatists utilize the "Sheldon grading scale." Despite some complaints of "too many grades," expert coin graders acknowledge and appreciate the wide range of attributes between grades.

STRIKE:

This method involves tracing or scribbling a drawing or a sign onto a blank surface. Depending on its design, a coin's strike can be mild or strong. The "Type II gold dollar" is an example of this, as both sides (obverse and reverse) have the greatest strike and are perfectly aligned. As a result, these styles necessitate feeble strikes.

Except when a coin is part of a series whose value is connected to a strike, the strike is not a critical component in determining the coin's grade.

SURFACE AREA CONSERVATION ON THE COIN:

The number of coin markings and where they are placed are important factors determining the grade. While there is no established procedure for determining the number of coin markings that determine its grade, there are various regulatory parameters for the significance of a scratch's area or location.

For example, a coin with a deep scratch that is well hidden on the reverse will not be penalized harshly. However, it would be penalized far more if the identical scratch were made on a conspicuous or noticeable key point on the front, such as the Statue of Liberty's cheek.

LUSTER VS. PATINA:

The surface of a coin can have a variety of textures, depending on the design, the metal used, and the "mint of origin." Satiny, prooflike, wintry, and semi-prooflike textures are all possible. When evaluating the coin's surface area for a grade, two factors must be considered: the amount of original skin that remains intact, as well as the location and number of marks. Luster is extremely important for determining whether a coin is circulated or uncirculated. A coin in Mint State is free of abrasion and wear, and its brilliance should not have significant fractures.

COLOR:

Determining the color of a coin is subjective and varies from one collector to another. For instance, a "gold coin" with a greenish-gold color may be unattractive to one collector but appealing to another. Gold, being an inert metal, is less likely to change color compared to silver or copper. Nonetheless, some gold coins may exhibit full-scale colors. Most US gold coins have been cleaned or dipped, resulting in the loss of their original color. However, experienced coin collectors prefer coins that have retained their original hue. Finding the first coins in a series is a challenging task for collectors in many instances.

ATTRACTION OR APPEAL TO THE EYES:

"Eye appeal" is defined by strike, shine, color, and surface area marks. Keep in mind that a coin with great "eye appeal" may be strong in one quality, such as luster, but weak in another, such as hue. Even if a coin is unfavorable in one aspect but adequate in all others, it can nevertheless be classified as "second-rate" in terms of "eye appeal." Understanding how to grade a coin is essential for determining the value or price of a coin that one is buying or selling. So, if you're new to coin collecting, make sure to get the advice of an experienced collector while buying or selling your coins.

LOOK:

When you first start collecting nickels, you'll notice that some are worn out, and others appear to be brand new. As you might expect, the condition of a coin impacts its worth. So, to determine value, we need a reference point.

The "Red Book" provides general values for each coin type based on a condition for each coin series that it defines. The illustration below, taken from the Red Book, depicts the grades or conditions of the Jefferson Nickel, which is quite useful for beginners. It serves as a guide to determining the condition of the nickels you find. A standard has been devised to assist us in determining the condition or grade. A numeric value is assigned to coins on a 70-point grading system. It's known as the "Sheldon Scale." The Sheldon Scale has grades ranging from Poor (P-1) to Perfect Mint State (MS-70.) Grades are typically assigned at significant locations along this scale, with the following being the most common:

POOR (P-1): Identifiable only by date and mintmark; otherwise, it's a shambles.

FAIR (FR-2): Nearly smooth, but without the damage that Poor coins have.

GOOD (G-4): Inscriptions have faded to the point where they blend into the rims in some spots; details are mostly removed.

VERY GOOD (VG-8): A little weathered, but all primary design elements are visible, albeit faintly. There isn't much in the way of core detail.

FINE (F-12): The item is worn, yet the wear is even, and the overall design details are prominent. Rims are almost completely separated.

VERY FINE (VF-20): - Moderately weathered, although with finer details. If present, all letters of LIBERTY should be readable. Rims that are full and clean.

EXTREMELY FINE (EF-40): Lightly used; all devices are visible, with the primary ones being bold.

UNCIRCULATED (AU-50): Slight evidence of wear on high points; contact markings possible; little eye appeal.

VERY SELECTIVE (AU-58): The tiniest traces of wear, no major contact marks, nearly full shine, and good eye appeal.

MINT STATE BASAL (MS-60): Strictly uncirculated, an unattractive coin with no sheen, visible contact marks, and so on.

ACCEPTABLE MINT STATE (MS-63): Uncirculated, but with touch marks and nicks, a slightly reduced shine, and a generally pleasing appearance. The strike is fair to the poor.

MINT STATE CHOICE (MS-65): Uncirculated with a bright luster, few contact marks, and great eye appeal. The strike rate is higher than usual.

MINT STATE PREMIUM QUALITY (MS-68): Uncirculated with perfect brilliance, no obvious contact marks to the naked eye, and exceptional eye appeal. Uncirculated with perfect luster, no visible contact markings to the naked eye, and exceptional eye appeal. The strike is beautiful and crisp.

MINT STATE ALL-BUT-PERFECT (MS-69): This coin is considered to be in uncirculated condition, displaying perfect luster, a sharp and attractive strike, and an exceptional eye appeal. Although it may contain tiny imperfections that are visible only under 8x magnification, such as those found in the planchet, striking, or contact markings, it is otherwise flawless.

MINT STATE PERFECT (MS-70): This is the perfect coin. The strike is sharp, exactly centered, and on a new planchet, with no minute imperfections discernible at 8x magnification. The luster is bright, rich, and unique, with excellent eye appeal. A simpler version might be more useful: grading companies frequently certify valuable coins worth $100 or more. Certified coins sell significantly more than uncertified ones because they assure both the vendor and the buyer that they are genuine. Purchasing certified coins ensure that we will receive what we pay for. However, there are a few verified fakes out there.

Let's look at some nickels and figure out what grade or condition they are in. The second pillar from the right is practically gone in the Red Book description for a VG-8 Very Good coin, as is the situation for the piece below. The remaining three pillars are visible but worn, indicating that this piece is very good or possibly Fine. According to the Red Book, an AU-50 coin about uncirculated displays indications of mild wear only on the design's high points. Only half of the mint luster remains. Take note of the pristine brilliance.

BOOK 3 - How to Start

Chapter 1

Tools and Method to Collect Coins

Coin collectors are well-known for their extensive understanding of precious metals. The explanation for this is straightforward. Many coins are silver or gold, and collectors are familiar with these metals, and this offers them a competitive advantage. They are familiar with counterfeit coins and false gold and silver, and they are knowledgeable about the worth of silver and gold coins. If you want to improve your precious metals knowledge, you should learn more about coins, particularly bullion coins. The key to success is knowledge.

Suppose you understand what a rare coin is and how to value one. In that case, you'll be in a lot better position to make investment decisions based on facts rather than habits, market trends, or aggressive salespeople's recommendations. This is a great place in the book to look at the tools you'll need to be a successful coin collector. Tools will be explained, why they're needed, how much they cost, and how to get them.

6.1 Tools for Coin Collection:

As your interest in coin collecting grows, you'll want to invest in some coin collecting gear and tools to help you put your collection together. While not exhaustive, the following items will help you become a more efficient and thorough coin collector:

- Nitrile gloves or any pair of gloves

- Jewelry loupe,
- A gram scale,
- A magnet,
- A digital microscope
- Reference books related to coin collection

These instruments are required for the coin collection. Because sometimes coins are so filthy, they are handled using nitrile gloves. They're useful when you're looking at many coins at once. You'll be surprised at how filthy they become after touching coins. Powder-free gloves are advisable. They come in a variety of sizes, so choose wisely. You'll be glad you did if you order 100. They are available in black and blue. When it comes to weighing money, a gram scale is a must-have. The capacity of these little scales is 8 ounces. Certain coins must be weighed to determine authenticity, metal content, and mistake types. Make sure the scale you buy is accurate to the hundredth of a gram.

A powerful magnet is utilized to identify counterfeit coins. Even if something doesn't stick to the magnet, it could still be false gold, fake silver, or a counterfeit coin. If someone tries to sell you a gold or silver coin and it adheres to the magnet, you know it's not genuine.

COIN MAGNIFIERS & LOUPES MAGNIFIER LOUPE

Every numismatist should own a star magnifier. These are necessary for determining a coin's worth, finding flaws and problems, checking for error coins, and discovering counterfeits. It's both practical and sensible to have a solid magnifier at home and a pocket magnifying or jeweler's loupe on the go. The majority of collectors prefer magnification of 10x to 20x.

REFERENCE BOOKS FOR COIN COLLECTION

To identify your coins and determine their value, you'll also need a reference book. If you're interested in collecting coins, you'll want to have at least one book that covers the basics like mintmarks and dates as well as notable varieties. Further reading on various related topics, such as how to detect counterfeits or different die varieties, can be extremely beneficial. Prices and news will be more up-to-date in periodicals. By helping you avoid making poor decisions, good reference books can pay for themselves many times over. Experts regard this list of references as a good starting point.

One of the following options might be a good fit for you:

RED BOOK - A GUIDEBOOK OF UNITED STATES COINS: This is the standard price guide for U.S. coins from the colonial era, as presented in the brochure. Collectors can expect to pay up to these prices for specific coins from a vendor. To learn everything there is to know about coin collecting, pick up a copy of this book. There should be a copy in every collection, and it is released annually.

STANDARD CATALOG OF WORLD COINS: The values of coins from the 20th century are available in this catalog. This is a great resource for learning about different world coins.

COIN COLLECTORS SURVIVAL MANUAL: Coin collectors will find a wealth of new information in this book written by a coin expert. Coin collecting topics have been discussed amusingly.

MANAGEMENT OF COINS

When handling coins, you must be cautious about how you hold and manipulate them. When holding a coin, I strongly advise you to invest in a pair of soft cotton gloves. Also, if you're not wearing gloves, always grasp the coin along the edges rather than on the face. The coin can be damaged by dirt and grease from the skin. If you don't want to handle the coin, a fine pair of coin tongs might come in handy. A beautiful padded tray is also helpful in sorting coins and laying out your collection for display. Of course, a plain towel can suffice as well.

1.2 COLLECTING METHOD AND APPROACHES

To be honest, there is no correct or incorrect technique to collect coins. Because this is a hobby for most people, the regulations should never be taken seriously. Sure, there are some things to be aware of and keep in mind.

Beyond that, though, you have complete control over how you acquire and organize your coins. If you stay informed and keep your eyes peeled, you can put together a collection of coins that are becoming increasingly valuable both in terms of their intrinsic value and in terms of what you previously had in your collection.

Many novice coin collectors begin by evaluating a larger collection and then reducing it down to what they are most interested in. Give yourself time and patience because it's difficult to know exactly what you want right away, especially if this is all new to you. Nobody is pressuring you into doing anything; these coins have been around for hundreds, if not thousands, of years, and if there's anything we can learn from them, it's that patience is golden.

If you're looking for some ideas on how to collect and organize your collection, consider the following suggestions:

- Sort them into denominations. This implies that you will combine all of a currency's distinct denominations. You'll probably start with a shorter time range, but if you find that this strategy appeals to you more than others, you can easily expand to decades or even entire eras.
- Sort them into categories. You can even limit yourself to simply collecting a specific sort of coin within a given denomination. You can also expand to other denominations if you want to.
- Sort them by the date they were collected. This means that you'll be collecting coins of the same denomination from several years. For example, you could begin by collecting all of the denominations from the year you were born until now.
- Then you can elaborate as you see fit. Sort them according to the date and mintmark combination. This can be more expensive because it instantly makes the coins you seek rarer– and so more expensive.
- Sort them into years. You might want to collect all the coins issued in the year you were born, for example. You can make this a decade-long project, or simply collect pennies from all around the world from the year you were born.
- Sort them into categories. This is a wonderful way to get started with coin collecting, and it may even be interesting for kids. For example, you might decide to collect all coins with presidents on them from the United States first, then the rest of the globe.
- Sort them according to the mintmark. This may be a little more challenging for a beginner due to the rarity of particular mintmarks, but it is not impossible.

- Gather them by chance. Many collectors, believe it or not, are anxious to get all of the errors from a certain period or currency. Why don't you do it as well?
- Sort them according to their rarity. As a rule, this will be more expensive because all of the coins you'll want to add to your collection are likely to be scarce already and thus expensive too.
- Sort them into countries. Country-based coin collections, like themed collections, can be a lot of fun for youngsters since they get to learn about different parts of the world.
- Sort them by time period. You might focus your coin collection on a specific period in history if you are fascinated by or attached to it. For example, you could amass all World War I coins from the United States and/or the rest of the world.
- Sort them into groups based on their design. Some people sort and collect coins based on the main design theme. For example, you can come across collections dedicated solely to animals, flowers, or sports.
- Sort them according to the metal they're made of. If you set your sights on gold or silver coins, for example, this may be more expensive, but the good news is that your collection can grow indefinitely as you set new goals. For example, you may start with all silver coins released in the United States up to a given period and then broaden your attention to the entire world. You can also extend the time span of your interest and then move to non-US currencies.

At the end of the day, it's up to you to determine how you want to store your coins. I honestly believe you should be having fun with this, so don't focus on one strategy just because it appears to provide a higher and faster return on investment.

Coin collection is a long-term game, so have some fun while you're at it. Furthermore, while most collecting methods can provide good earnings, there's no need to compulsively focus on one method just because it's more profitable or because someone else tells you that you must collect coins a certain way.

CHAPTER 2

PRESERVE AND PROTECT THE COIN COLLECTION

Handling and storage of coins should be practiced. Purchase a safe deposit box to protect your coins from loss and to keep them safe from floods, fires, and thieves, among other things. Excessive heat, sunshine, and humidity should be avoided. Coin flips and coin folders are also available to help you display your coin. Handle them with gloves on. Keep a magnifying lens handy to examine for minute flaws and counterfeit evidence, as damaged coins are worthless. As a result, handle and store it with caution.

Avoiding wear or introducing substances that might cause spots or color changes is a cardinal rule for all coin collectors. Try to keep your coins away from direct human contact. This implies that you should not handle the coins with your bare hands. Fingerprints are the arch-enemy of the collectible coin. It's also critical to avoid allowing one coin to come into contact with another, as this can cause nicks and scratches. Remove coins from storage containers only when necessary to avoid them being ruined.

Uncirculated or Proof coins should only be handled on edge, as even a minor fingerprint can lower the coin's grade and thus its value. Proof coins have been struck two or more times with polished dyes on an equally polished planchet, and they are legal tender in the same way that regular coins are.

The US government packages coins for sale to coin collectors as uncirculated mint sets. Pick up collectible coins by the rim while wearing clean white cotton or surgical gloves. A face mask is also recommended to avoid small particles of moisture from causing undesirable spots. Sneezing or coughing near coins can leave marks on the coin, causing it to deteriorate.

COINS FROM THE UNITED STATES MINT:

For normal handling, coin holders are sufficient protection. If you must remove the coin from the holder and place it on a clean, soft surface, such as a velvet pad, do so. It's the perfect surface for managing valuable numismatic materials, and it's a must-have accessory. A clean, soft cloth can be used for coins of lesser value. To prevent scratches, avoid dragging coins across any surface. Even wiping with a clean cloth can cause scratches, lowering the item's value.

CLEANING AND MAINTAINING YOUR COINS:

While it is desirable to keep the environment clean, cleaning the coins is not recommended. Although a gleaming coin may appear attractive, a collectible coin must retain its original appearance. The numismatic value can be drastically reduced by cleaning it, and there are only a few options to enhance the coin's appearance.

You may end up causing more harm than good. Cleaning collectible coins unnecessarily lowers their value and cost. A coin's patina develops over time and is an important part of its overall essence and history, reflecting a value far greater than its face value. Its value can be reduced by up to 90%

if you remove it! Collectors prize coins with appealing patinas because they act as shields for the coin's surface.

Like any other form of art restoration, cleaning coins is best left to the pros. They know how to use the most effective techniques while maintaining the coin's value. If you think you need to clean a tarnished coin, you just found it's a bad plan, and its best if you don't touch the coin. Toning is a natural process that results in the color shift you see. If allowed to progress naturally and produce appealing results, it can also add to the coin's value.

The atoms on the coin's surface react chemically, usually with sulfur compounds, to produce toning. It can't be reversed, but there are "dips" where you can remove molecules from the coin's surface. However, keep in mind that professionals should only do this. There are a few guidelines to follow when it comes to cleaning coins that you've acquired, found, bought, or inherited.

1. If you don't know the numismatic value, don't clean it. If you're unsure whether or not something is valuable, don't clean it. It's best to leave coins untouched in their original location, and it is preferable to err on the side of caution rather than risking the coin. They should be kept in holders made specifically for this purpose. Coin collectors and dealers prefer coins in their original state, so don't change them. Cleaning is more likely to cause harm than good.

2. You must take the coins to an expert coin cleaning service because you cannot clean the coins yourself. They use a "dipping" technique to clean the coins properly while preserving their value. This is critical, particularly if the coin's date and details are corroded. A professional will be able to prevent or reduce further coin damage.

3. If you discover a coin that needs to be cleaned, use the least damaging method possible. Use no harsh chemicals, sulfuric acid, polishing cloths, vinegar, abrasive pastes, or other devices that give the coin a smooth and shiny finish. Start with lower-value coins and work your way up to higher-value coins.

4. Because cleaning is such a big deal in coin collecting, you must tell a buyer if a coin has been cleaned.

SOAKING COINS

VARIOUS TYPES OF COINS:

Cleaning uncirculated coins will destroy the mint luster. Gold coins should be carefully cleaned in a neat, lukewarm, bubbly purified liquid, using a cottony fiber wash-down fabric or a simple tooth scrub. Because gold is smooth metal, it must be handled with caution to avoid disfiguring or scratching.

SILVER COINS: Do not clean any valuable silver coins. Some silver coins have a blue-green or violet oil-like tarnish, dirt, minerals, or other residues that add to their beauty and should be left alone. Ammonia, rubbing alcohol, vinegar, or acetone-based polish remover must clean dark silver coins, and rubbing or polishing them is not a good idea.

If required, immerse copper coins in grape oil to clean them, and olive oil can suffice if none is available. In no way should you try to rub them. However, it may take a few weeks to a year for results to appear, so be patient. Cleaning nickel coins is best done with a gentle toothbrush and warm, soapy distilled water. Use ammonia diluted 3 to 1 with distilled water to clean heavily tarnished nickel coins.

KEEPING YOUR COINS SAFE:

To preserve the numismatic worth of your coins, you must store them carefully. Depending on the worth of the coin you're saving, you'll need the appropriate type of holder. You can save your series or type collection in commercially available folders and albums. If you're going to use paper envelopes, be sure the materials are specifically designed for storing money, especially high-value coins, because sulfur or other chemicals in the paper might induce a reaction and affect the coin's color.

Plastic flips manufactured of Mylar and acetate are suitable for long-term storage, but they might harm the coin if not inserted and withdrawn gently due to their hardness and brittleness. Polyvinyl chloride (PVC) was employed to make "soft" flips; however, it deteriorated over time and left the coinages with dreadful results. On the coins, PVC gave them an emerald hue. In the United States, PVC reverses are no longer produced or sold. Tubes can accommodate multiple coins of the same size and, if not moved, appear to take up the majority of the space in distributed coinages and higher-grade coins. Hard plastic carriers, which do not contain dangerous elements and can prevent money from scratches and other physical damage, are recommended for more precious coins.

COLLECTIBLE COINS:

Slabs, which provide good protection for more expensive coins, can be used. Slabs are individual coin holders made of hermetically sealed hard plastic. One disadvantage is the cost, and you won't be able to access the coin if you need it immediately.

A dry atmosphere with low humidity and little temperature variation is essential for long-term storage. Moisture in the air causes oxidation; therefore, you should avoid it as much as possible. Although eliminating oxidation will not decrease the coin's worth, it will improve its appearance. Silica gel packets should be placed in the coin storage area to control ambient moisture. Even if you keep your collection in a safe deposit box, you should always check on it regularly. If difficulties arise due to improper storage, you can intervene before major harm occurs.

SECURING YOUR COLLECTION FROM FIRE AND THEFT:

Any of your possessions will always be at risk of being destroyed by fire or stolen. There are, however, some steps you may take to limit them, just as you would protecting your house or automobile against them. Keep in mind that most homeowner policies do not cover coins or other numismatic arti-facts. However, a rider is typically available for a fee. A separate policy can also be purchased. Consider becoming a member of the American Numis-matic Association (ANA), which offers coin collection insurance to its mem-bers. Make sure your collection's catalog is kept separate from the coins. Please keep track of where you got each coin, its condition, and how much you spent on it. It's also a good idea to take individual close-up shots of each coin. Get a professional appraisal using a Blue Book or Red Book? The in-surance company requires the appraisal documentation.

Safes keep your valuables safe from theft, fire, dust, water, and other ele-ments that could harm them. They provide some safeguarding for your coins. Some safes are fire-resistant but not theft-resistant. Although some safes prevent burglars, they are not fireproof. Even if the flames do not con-tact your coins, they can be damaged or destroyed. The heat may cause them to melt. Humidity is another factor to consider when storing coins in a safe. Oxidation, which is hazardous for coins, will occur high. Thirty percent rel-ative humidity is the best setting (RH). The ambient RH where the safe is positioned determines the RH within the safe. Fortunately, the majority of modern safes are well-insulated and well-built. Packets of silica gel can help to minimize humidity.

If you decide to keep your collection at home, make sure you buy a safe that can withstand fire, dampness, and theft. Take precautions to deter or pre-vent a burglar from breaking into your home. Lighting should be adequate, and locks should be solid and robust. More helpful hints can be obtained by approaching law enforcement officers. Being discreet about your coin col-lecting hobby is one approach to protect your investment from theft. Your personal information may end up in the hands of the wrong person if you share it with many people. Having any numismatic promotional materials addressed to a post office box rather than your home can benefit.

BOOK 4 – WORLDWIDE COLLECTION

CHAPTER 1

GET COINS FROM DIFFERENT SOURCES

1.1 WHERE TO LOCATE COINS?

Coin collecting is a fun pastime. First and foremost, have a glance in your pocket, and it is the ideal location for coin collecting. Look before spending money with your pocket change, and separate the attractive coins. Coins can also be obtained via various sources, including coin-stores, coin shows, the internet and mail orders, and fellow collectors.

FINDING RARE AND COLLECTIBLE COINS:

For many people, coin collecting began as a recreational activity and inspired more people to start collecting coins. There are many places to start your coin collection if you are one of those people who want to acquire coins.

COIN SHOPS:

These coin shops are great places to learn about coins and coin collecting. These coin shops may be pricey since they want to sell their coins for a profit. You can receive great rates for your coins if you have enough knowledge and someone who knows a lot about coin collecting on your side.

COIN SHOWS:

There are instances when a display of numerous coin sellers will be set up in your local mall. These will allow you to view their collection and allow you to purchase a handful of them at a reduced price due to competition. You'll almost certainly see several new coins that are available for purchase and would make excellent additions to your collection. These coin exhibits are wonderful for collectors and coin lovers who want to see rare and diffi-cult-to-find coins.

WEB SITES/MAIL ORDERS:

There are numerous dealers worldwide, and most of them have websites where you can pay by mail order or using an online payment system like PayPal. You should do your homework on these companies and study their rules carefully to ensure that you can get your money back if you have prob-lems with the coin you received. There is certainly a slew of fraudulent web-sites vying for your money for every genuine website. Before paying anyone online, you should get some feedback and ensure you don't give out pass-words or PINs.

SOME GOOD SITES TO BUY COINS:

www.vcoins.com is a good place to start. There are some fine coins on this site, and dealers must follow a code of conduct. Coins from the United States, ancient coins, and foreign coins are all listed.

You can subscribe to their free newsletter by filling out the form below.

With the addition of a new coin collectibles section to Amazon, it has ex-panded its coin offers. You can check through: http://www.amazon.com/Collectible-Coins/b?ie=UTF8&node=9003130011.

There's a search bar and a lot of category options. There are two other coin auction houses/dealers that should be mentioned. These are the two most important coin firms globally in terms of auctioning valuable coins, and they also sell coins, usually of high value.

Heritage Auctions is the largest coin dealer and auction company globally and one of the best. You can buy from their site www.ha.com.

Single coins and select sets are available for purchase at reasonable prices. This is a good site to look for unusual coins, and it's also a good place to sell your precious coins.

Stacks Bowers (http://www.stacksbowers.com/) is another well-known coin dealer and auction company. This website allows you to purchase coins.

Coin Community (http://www.coincommunity.com/) is an excellent forum and resource for locating coins.

Your local coin club is also an excellent place to go if you want to buy high-quality coins from individuals you know. Keep in mind that you can find some nice coin ads on Craigslist.

FLEA MARKETS:

Markets where buying and selling occur are unexpected places to find rare coins. However, due to a lack of knowledge about how coins are valued, these markets often have different price perceptions. Though you may find expensive coins, you could also come across unique coins among the piles of coins, making it a worthwhile experience. Flea market sellers are typically interested in making a quick sale, so buying in bulk can often result in discounts. Consider purchasing other items to receive a coin as a bonus.

AUCTIONS:

If you are seeking to acquire highly rare coins, the optimal place to explore is an auction. Auctions are the sole venues where one may discover individuals selling their most valuable and exceptional coins. Many of these auctions are now held online, and most sellers aim to find the highest bidders. Nonetheless, it is essential to bear in mind that some of these merchants may be scammers who will not provide a reasonable value for the price paid.

Prior to attempting to purchase a rare coin from an online auction, it is advisable to educate oneself about these coins and their approximate worth.

There are a couple of nice auction tools available:

Ezsniper www.ezs niper.com/index.php3 works great, and you receive three free auction bids before paying 1% for any auctions you win after that.

There are also other free sniping programs with decent reviews:

http://www.gixen.com/index.php

https://www.jbidwa tcher.com/

www.auctionshadow.com is another tool that can assist you in analyzing a seller's comments.

1.2 COIN COLLECTION FROM OTHER COUNTRIES:

Coin collectors frequently have the same coins that they would like to sell for a lower price than the market value. The only problem is that finding another coin collector like you is difficult. Online groups, forums, and neighborhood groups are the greatest places to look if you have one. When you want to start a coin collection, the ideal people to talk to are other coin collectors. They may be able to make recommendations, offer discounts, and even present you with a few of their coins to help you get started with your collection. Like any other investment, Coin collecting is a long-term commitment, and they deteriorate, although other coins may rise in value. The greatest way to make money from coin collecting is to regularly keep up with the latest news and coin values. These will not only help you avoid being duped by various vendors, but they will also teach you how to price a coin without using a catalog.

SPANISH COINS:

Spain had one edge over all other governments controlling territory in North America in the 1700s: it possessed Mexico and the majority of South America. These areas' huge silver mines gave Spain an abundance of the popular white metal, mostly converted into coins before being sent to European treasuries. Spanish coins were so well accepted in world trade that they were accepted in every country at the period, including the British North American colonies, where they were highly valued and accepted by everyone, including local governments who took them as tax payments. The Eight Reales or Piece of Eight, a big silver piece that served as the standard for British and American dollar coins and was used and accepted as money in the United States until 1857, was the most popular coin of the time.

FRENCH COINS:

The French controlled a large amount of land in the colonies, both within what would eventually become the United States, including the Louisiana Territory, and within what would eventually become Canada. As a result, when the French immigrated to America, they brought a few pennies with them. Other coins, designed expressly for use in French colonies, were underweight and unpopular. However, being realists, the colonists accepted any money, including any of France's silver and copper pieces.

VIRGINIAN COPPERS:

King George III approved the coinage of copper halfpennies for Virginia of the United Kingdom in 1773. These royal coins, known as Virginia coppers, showed a bust of George on one side and his coat of arms on the other. The coins were made in England and then shipped to Virginia to be used by colonists.

BIBLICAL COINS:

The Roman denarius, the Jewish shekel, and the widow's mite are all mentioned in the Bible. Something about these coins elicits a specific reaction in today's coin enthusiasts. Coins are the only concrete remembrance of biblical figures, locations, and events when it comes down to them. When you hold a tiny widow's mite in your fingers, you understand how much such a small coin may represent. And you start to wonder if you're holding the coin that the older woman offered as an offering.

BYZANTINE EMPIRE COINS:

The Roman Empire crumbled gradually but steadily, and the Byzantine Empire, centered in Constantinople, took its place in the West. Anastasius introduced a new copper currency called a follis, worth 40 nummi, beginning in A.D. 498.

The Byzantines also produced exquisite gold and silver coins. Byzantine coins are noted for their religious symbolism, which frequently incorporates crosses, representations of Christ, and other Christian symbols. Like earlier Roman coins, many Byzantine coins feature depictions of the emperors. Byzantine coins, like many other antique coins, are relatively inexpensive.

Many gold coins are available for less than $500, and Byzantine bronzes are frequently available for less than $40.

CIRCULATED U.S. WHEAT CENTS 1958:

Dealers buy several outdated 1940 or later for less than 2 cents each piece. Some of the earlier dates are value more from a few pennies to hundreds of dollars, so checking a pricing guide is a good plan if you have one. In 1959, the wheat stalk reversal was replaced with the contemporary design. A handful of wheat cents is scarce, yet it is worth a lot of money. The first time this style was used was in 1909. Any cents that are in good condition are worth a lot of money. Several of the more scarce 1909 ranges are worth hundreds, if not thousands, of dollars. There are also a few more rare dates in the series. One thousand nine hundred thirty-two cents and a few Second World War error coins are also worth a lot of money.

1943 Steel Pennies

In 1943 only Zinc-plated steel cents were struck. In early 1999, a nationally syndicated radio broadcast incorrectly said that these coins are valuable and rare. More than a billion coins were produced but in 1943 cent struck on a standard bronze planchet is rare and valuable.

Any 1943 cent that appears to be bronze must be examined to discover if it pulls towards a magnet. If that's the case, it's a copper-plated steel cent, and 1943 steel cents could be worth as little as 5 cents. Uncirculated prices do not apply to steel-cents that have been "re-processed" and given a new zinc layer.

Silver Quarters, Dimes, and Halves:

United States dimes, half dollars, and quarters minted before 1964 are 91% silver and contain 0.723 ounces of silver every dollar of face value. Because a small amount of metal worn away due to circulation, 0.716 ounces/dollar is commonly used to calculate approximately the amount of silver still present.

Even if the coin is a common date, its silver content makes it worth more than its face-value. The quantity varies depending on the price of silver in the Kitco Inc. area provides precious metal area prices. Multiply the current silver spot price by 0.715 and the total face value. If the area is $5.00 per ounce, the bullion value for a $120 face value is $5.00 x .715 x 120 = $429. Many uncirculated silver coins and circulated silver coins could fetch a sum over the silver value. Look through a pricing guide to see the better pricing dates. Between 1965 and 1970, the silver content of half dollars in the United States was 40%.

SILVER DOLLARS:

Before 1935, silver dollars in the United States were prepared with 0.76 ounces of silver. These coins are admired among collectors and can often be sold for more than their silver value, and high grades and less common dates could fetch a lot more money.

SUSAN B. ANTHONY DOLLARS:

It's probably worth a dollar if you got it as a change. Proof S.B.A dollars have a higher value; however, proof coins rarely circulate.

BICENTENNIAL QUARTERS, DOLLARS AND HALVES:

There are so many of these coins; they're frequently only worth face value. A few dealers pay about 12% more than face value for weakly circulated bicentennial coin rolls and a little more for uncirculated ones. Special 40 percent silver bicentennial coins were made and sold to collectors to commemorate the Bicentennial. The lack of copper on the brink easily identifies them. Although they have a higher worth than face value, they are unlikely to be discovered in circulation.

SILVER DOLLAR TYPE SET

MORGAN DOLLAR   PEACE DOLLAR   SEATED LIBERTY DOLLAR

The Royal Wedding Of Princess Diana And Prince Charles Is Commemorated On A Coin:

Many British Commonwealth countries generated millions. They are now priced somewhere from $5 to $25.

Mules or a Coin with 2 Heads and 2 Tails:

These items are "novelty" items commonly known as magician's coins, with a few exceptions. Burrowing 1 coin and cutting another to fit within is how they're made. A seam could be found along the internal rim edge on one side. They have no value to coin collectors because they are modified coins.

Nonetheless, in 2000, a tiny number of real mistake coins recognized as "mules" were discovered. A mule is generated when dies for diverse denominations are matched with striking the two-coin sides. The mules that were recently discovered are:

- A single 1999 Lincoln cent with a reverse of the Roosevelt dime exists.
- At least 6 Sacagawea "golden dollars" featuring George Washington on the obverse, anticipated for a state quarter
- A single 1869 Indian penny struck using 2 obverse dies.

If a person have one of these exceedingly rare coins, a dealer or collector in your area may be able to aid you in determining whether it is genuine. Once the coin has been professionally validated, you can consign it to an auction to find the greatest price.

A Coin Un-Struck:

Planchets or blanks that have not been struck are rather common. Many are available for a few dollars or less at retail.

A Mis-Struck Coin:

There are different types of eye-catching errors. In addition, many coins appear to be rare because they've been altered after striking. The modified coins are worthless for coin collectors. Genuine striking errors have a wide variety of prices. Small errors, such as an elevated fracture, will usually result in little or no first-class. Clips, incomplete planchets, and off-center strikes usually sell for a few bucks.

Uncommon, exceptional errors could fetch hundreds of dollars. The first step is determining the value of an unusual-looking coin and examined it by different experts.

BOOK 5 - FROM HOBBY TO BUSINESS

CHAPTER 1

COIN COLLECTION FROM HOBBY TO BUSINESS

1.1 COIN COLLECTING AS A BEGINNER

Collecting coins is a fun pastime. As a beginner, you might begin with little steps. Collect a coin and learn as much as you can about the coin's past, history, and worth.

Things are also possible to begin putting it together. Gather the coins that you enjoy. For example, you can select or collect coins based on their appealing design or a compelling backstory. To learn more about the coin's history, you can use the internet. Because coin collection is neither a race nor a competition, it must be done gradually and patiently. If you're thinking about buying a coin, look into its history and value. Please don't buy anything right away; instead, wait for a period when you'll be able to get it or pick it up at a reasonable cost.

PUTTING TOGETHER YOUR COLLECTION:

The simplest way to start collecting coins is to focus on those currently in circulation. You might, however, want to extend out into coins that are no longer in use. Along with coins, dealers and their coin stores can be wonderful sources of information. Take part in a few coin shows. You can buy from many different sellers at the same time. The selection will undoubtedly be superior to that of most stores, and you may be able to negotiate better prices. You can purchase coins via the mail from a variety of sellers. Unfortunately, receiving a faulty or over-graded coin from certain mail-order companies is all too prevalent.

It's important to ensure that the seller has a reasonable return policy before making a purchase. Once you receive the coins, carefully inspect them to ensure that they meet your expectations. If you're uncertain, seek a second opinion from an experienced collector or dealer, and consider visiting them if necessary. You can also explore auction options, including live auctions and those conducted online, such as on eBay. Major specialist auction houses in larger cities often promote auctions featuring the rarest and most valuable coins.

Bids during these auctions are significantly lower or higher than values for similar coins from other sources. To prevent excessive spending, look at prices in stores, mail order advertisements, or online and limit your bids to those costs.

Antiques, estate, and other collectibles auctions frequently feature common collector coins. Typically, the coins are over-graded, have flaws that the auctioneer does not bring out, or have inflated pricing. You can trade or buy from another collector, but it isn't easy to discover other collectors who have the same what you're looking for. If this happens, you might be able to negotiate a better deal. You can also use coin collector message boards to connect with other collectors.

Browse around or use Google to find them. Coins are frequently available at antique shows, flea markets, artisan fairs, and other events where they are not the major attraction. Because there is little to no competition for the vendor and many potential buyers unfamiliar with the hobby, these locations can shift and inflate prices. While the collector always wishes to judge the quality of potential purchases and the justice of their prices, more caution is essential in these situations.

COIN COLLECTING ACCESSORIES:

When collecting coins, one thing to think about is organizing and caring for them. Antique, ancient, or limited-edition coins are among the collected coins. These coins are made in various countries and have a high monetary worth.

A collector needs to know how to manage and care for them to maintain their original appearance and worth. Buying various coin accessories is usually one way to take care of coins. Coin accessories make a coin collection beautiful, structured, and care for and preserve the coins. When purchasing coin accessories, choosing the ones that will best meet the collector's demands is critical. Durability, affordability, and utility are just a few considerations to consider. Many coin accessories can be bought at antique stores and even on the internet.

Listed below are a few coin accessories to consider:

1. COIN BOXES

Coin boxes are the most popular coin accessories because they are extremely useful to collectors and experts. The sections in the box make it simple to locate the coins, and the compartments are also wide, allowing you more versatility in coin placement. The large compartments also allow the collector to handle the coins properly.

2. COIN ALBUMS

Coin albums are designed to hold coins, similar to regular albums, but with specific features for coin storage. The albums typically include a transparent cover for added protection and to prevent mishandling. Coin collectors can easily turn the pages without having to handle each coin individually, ensuring the safety of the coins.

3. HOLDERS OF COINS

Coin collectors who collect coins on their trips will benefit the most from coin holders. They enable coin collection mobility. Furthermore, the collector is not required to transport his complete collection, and he could only fit one coin into the coin holder. Coin holders keep coins safe and protect them from the many elements that can diminish their value.

On the market, there are a variety of coin accessories. Determine the accessory's primary function and whether it will meet your requirements. Prices will vary depending on how long the item will last. Before deciding on a coin accessory, do some research and price comparisons.

1.2 DOCUMENT YOUR COLLECTION

Do you say you don't have a coin catalog?

Why should I keep track of my coins?

You have a coin catalog that includes the date of purchasing, the purchase amount, and who sold the coin to you, right?

Many coin collectors I know feel driven to keep track of their holdings. Others toss the pennies into a bag, box, or old Mason jar and set them aside. Keeping track of your coins is a crucial element of the pastime. The IRS requires you to keep your coin purchases and sales for taxation. When there are no records, the IRS may presume anything on the spot. The coin's worth is profit, so it's taxable. If you have, it's not a pretty picture. I've amassed a sizable collection, yet I haven't kept even the most basic records! Another reason to keep track of your coins is to assist your heirs.

If something were to happen to you, your estate would be a good place to start.

What if they don't have any records of a coin?

Will they have the necessary tools to liquidate the collection?

They don't have to if they don't want to. Keep a well-kept catalog of your coin collection to keep coins on track so they don't get sidetracked when it's time to get rid of the coins.

Cataloged Coins in a Variety of Ways:

Coin collectors know to utilize various strategies to keep track of their collections. Some people keep track of everything on regular 3x5 cards, and others utilize sophisticated coin-collecting software.

There is no one-size-fits-all solution for cataloging your coin collection. You should select a comfortable way for you to employ with your coins, and it should also be a way that you will utilize regularly. It's also crucial to maintain track of what you're doing.

This is the shortlist that I use for all of my projects.

- Collections
- Originating Country
- Mint's Year
- Denomination
- Grade

- Purchased Date

- Price of Purchase

- Date of Sale

- Price Reduced

If you buy and sell rolls frequently, you might wish to set up a column for "Quantity."

Another chance is that you'll get variation or mistake coins if you buy them, and I want to add that information in a column.

All you need is a notebook, a pen, and a straight edge to make the drawing.

There is a need for columns. Because almost everyone has a computer, you almost certainly have a spreadsheet. Microsoft Excel or possibly Open Office are examples of such applications. Either of these apps makes creating a comprehensive means of communication straightforward. You can keep track of your coin collection, as well as assess the value of your coins.

SOFTWARE FOR COIN COLLECTING:

Coin collecting software with an integrated database is the solution to arrange your collection. You can use a database to keep track of your coins and worth. There are several of them. Various software programs are available. Some are free, but the majority are fairly priced. Others are a little more costly. You get what you paid for, like with everything else. You could even use Microsoft Access, which is included in the package, to create your database. Microsoft Office premium editions are available.

To gather coins, the software should be:

- Simple to use.

- Intuitive.

- Simple to Keep Your Collections Organized.

- Availability of Current Pricing.

- Your coin values are automatically updated.

- Coin collecting software can save you time and make cataloging your collection easier.

Is it required of everyone? You're the only person who can help yourself.

Please respond to that. Using a basic spreadsheet to keep track of your coins could be your best option. One of the new things you've learned? It would help if you were cataloging. But the question is, do you have a coin collection?

1.3 How to Monetize Your Coin Collection Hobby?

Whether you started collecting coins as a hobby or investment, there may come a time when you consider selling your coins. It could be due to a personal financial need or to help a friend or relative, but it's unlikely that you're selling them because you've lost interest. Like any commodity, you expect a fair price and hope to make a profit, no matter how small. You have several options for selling your collection. One option is to go through a public auction, but keep in mind that most auction houses have a minimum consignment value. If your collection falls below this figure, you'll need to find another dealer who accepts lower-value coins and can quickly auction them for you. Another option is a personal sale, which can be the quickest but also the riskiest and most time-consuming. You'll need to approach several dealers and offer your coins for sale, hoping to find one who can give you a reasonable price. You could also put an ad in the newspaper, but be cautious of dubious offers that could come from dishonest people looking to take advantage of you. A third option is to have your coins consigned to a local dealer, but you should only do this if you have personal knowledge of the dealer's background. Ask if they are willing to accept the coins for a certain amount over which they can impose a markup. Most dealers will accept this since the markup is already a sure profit and they have no financial investment. For our purposes here, we will discuss the second option: personal sale. You first need to know exactly what you have in your collection and how much they are worth to you, the dealer, and the buyers. You need to know what you will be selling so you need to do some homework. The first task you must accomplish is to create an inventory of all your collection. You need to identify each coin to know how much each is worth and your entire collection. You may already have an idea, especially if you have purchased all of them. You might even think that based on your calculations of the price you paid when you acquired them plus a markup, you would be making a handsome profit, right? Besides, if you read coin-value magazines, you would know that a certain coin in your collection is worth this much. Well, it depends. Remember that the price you paid when you bought your coins and the price listed on those magazines are retail prices, not what a dealer would pay. Also, a lot of the value depends on the collection's condition. They would have to be checked for damage. The bottom line is, you will not receive what you expect, and it will be a lower amount. You can also refer to one of the references mentioned above, the "Official Red Book: A Guidebook of United States Coins." It can give you an idea of your coins' approximate range of value. Now you need to find a dealer who can appraise your coins correctly. Do some research and look at the background of several dealers you have in mind. You can find them at the website of the Professional Numismatic Guild (PNG). It would help you that the dealers are reputable members in good standing of the American Numismatic Association (ANA) or any known numismatic club. You may have to learn it the hard way, but at this point, you must make sure that the dealer you will finally choose is honest and will give you what your coins are worth. Once you have made your choice, take steps to contact the dealer. You can do this either by phone or email if they have one. When you contact them, identify yourself; inform them about your intention to sell your collection, and give them the inventory list you created earlier. If you are in luck, the dealer may accept your collection. If not, and the dealer is not interested in your collection because it is an average one, and they will not profit, you need to go to the next dealer on your list. The dealer who accepts your collection will make an offer which could sound very disappointing to you. The dealer will certainly not offer the price you were expecting but rather the wholesale price, which is much lower than the retail price. Remember that the price you had in mind is the retail price, the amount you are willing to pay for the coins. What the dealer will give you is the price that he will pay so that they can make a profit when your collection is sold. Also, the dealer reserves the right to revise the offer based on the actual condition of the coins. The dealer may not agree with the grade of the coins you had in mind and if the dealer is lower, expect a huge drop in the price offered. If, for one reason or another, you couldn't agree on a price that's reasonable to both of you, go to the next dealer on your list again. At one point in your search for the right dealer, you may want to consider offering your collection to an auction house. If your collection meets their criteria, you may be able to get a higher price. However, make sure you know the fees involved and do some math. You may or may not come out as the winner in this case. Assuming now that a written offer that is acceptable to you has been made and you have decided to sell, you can either have the buyer come to you or if the buyer is located far away, in another state or city perhaps, you can choose to send your collection through the mail. This can be risky, of course, but there are precautions you can take to ensure that the coins arrive safely at their doorsteps. Ensure that you package them very well, avoid loose coins that could jingle around the package, and advertise themselves as coins with value. Include an itemized list, too, so the buyer can readily check the items upon arrival. The USPS Priority Mail is a safe way to send them. Select the most economical mail option available to you. Have the coins insured for your protection and an additional fee for delivery confirmation?

A. the Finer Points of Selling Your Collection to better understand what has been discussed above, a closer look at the world of coin dealers is in order. Coin dealers come in two categories. There are the wholesaler and the retailer. The wholesaler is the one who seeks out new coins to bring into the marketplace. To do this, this type of dealer attends coin shows, auctions and some may even run advertisements to buy coins. Since this dealer sells the coins wholesale, you can expect them to lower prices. But as a coin collector, you can't just go to these dealers and buy from them. You go to the retailers to buy your coins. The retailers usually get the bulk of their coins from the wholesalers. They also attend coin shows, auctions, etc., but their primary customers who bring the money are the ordinary single coin buyers looking to start or complete their collection.

B. Wholesale Coin Prices Whether you are selling or buying coins, knowing the wholesale prices will help you transact with any dealer. This information can be obtained from the Coin Dealer Newsletter, more commonly known as the "Grey Sheet." This publication lists every important US coin's "bid" and "ask" prices. "Bid" price refers to what dealers will pay another dealer for coins. Ask" price refers to what dealers ask to buy or what they want their clients to pay them, which is usually higher than the bid price. When you call a dealer to buy coins; the dealer will quote you the "ask" price. But when you call to sell coins, the dealer will quote you the "bid" price, again usually lower now than the "ask' price. This is how dealers make money, just like any other commodity: buy low and sell high. Bear in mind, though, that these transactions are about wholesale selling, which means bulk orders and no single coins. Deals like this require a minimum quantity of coins to work. Do not expect dealers to pay you the "bid" prices listed in the Grey Sheet. This publication gives you enough idea, so you don't sell your collection worth $10,000 for $500. A lot of dealers would like that. Another point to consider about wholesale coin pricing is that the more valuable the coin is, the smaller the profit margin in terms of percentage. For example, a coin that sells for $10,000 can be bought by a dealer for $9,000. The dealer is sure to make a handsome profit if it is sold at the original price. However, the dealer's investment is left tied up and the coin stuck in the inventory for a long time before a coin buyer can come up with the $10,000, a hefty amount.

C. When selling a coin collection, you have two options: selling the coins as a complete set or selling them individually. Each option has its pros and cons depending on the effort you're willing to invest. Selling the coins as a complete set may not fetch the expected value for each coin, but it ensures that you can sell the entire collection. If you have a complete set, it's best to leave it as it is, knowing its value and comparing it with the bids you receive. Although you may get a lower amount, you save time and effort by avoiding the task of selling coins individually. Selling the entire collection is a less time-consuming and labor-intensive way to sell them. You can bring them to the dealer or coin shop of your choice with an inventory, making it easy for them to evaluate your collection. You can also opt to sell cone coin at a time and make some more money from each coin. However, you can expect some coins to be left behind, especially those with lesser value. Selling one coin at a time involves so much effort than selling the entire collection at once. Thus, you must find the balance between what you hope to receive for the entire collection against what you will potentially earn if you sell them as individual coins. Remember that you need to spend many hours and leg work to sell them individually. Do not lower your prices until you exhaust all possibilities of getting a higher price and are sure no one else will buy your coins at your asking price. Your best bet is to concentrate on getting high bids for your highest value coins. If you sell your coins individually, you can maximize your profit by putting each coin in a 2X2 coin holder. Have the coin holders marked with the date and mintmark if the coins have it. If you don't know the grade and you have no idea how it is done, don't write the grade on them. Do not guess. If you want, create a separate list of the Grey Sheet or Red Book value for each coin. Placing the coins in its holder makes it a valued individual coin. If you go to a dealer and accept the whole lot, they will quote a price, but it could be higher than if you just let the coins bunched together in a folder. As individual coins, they appear to have much more value than grouped. A bonus for the dealer is that they need not put them in individual 2X2 holders as you have done it already. Put Those Bags and Purses Away You wouldn't want the dealer to think that you are squirreling his coins into your purse. Keep your hands free and open to view. This way, the dealer will not think you are doing something you shouldn't be doing. When you need to sit down, put your bag or purse on the back of your chair or the floor under the chair, never on your lap or in front of you. Again, the point here is to look at things from the dealer's point of view: you wouldn't want your customers dropping your coins onto their bags or purses, which is what the dealer will think if you put your bag in your lap or in front of you where you can drop a coin at a reasonable time. Pick the Best but Be Sure You Know Where You Picked It There is a term in the numismatic hobby that best describes how a collector finds a coin: cherry-picking. The term is based on the process of harvesting cherries where the selector is expected only to select the ripest and healthiest fruit. Applied to coin collecting, it is the art of buying the best coin possible for the least price. This means going through many coins in the box and finding the valuable one among worthless ones. But it often happens that some would forget where they picked up the coin and just put it back wherever they could. This results in confusion and embarrassment if the coin is not returned to its original container, especially if the coin's price is different, whether higher or lower, from where it originally came from. Beware: Bury Those Books and Checklists It is an acceptable practice to bring reference books like "the Red Book" so you can consult their pages and be properly informed about the prices. However, you should not bring them out when looking and handling the coins. Remember to consider this scene from the dealer's point of view again: you could easily slip coins between pages or slips of paper. Of course, you will not do that, but the dealer might think you will. So, don't let any coins near your books and papers. Show Me You're Hands! Please don't blame the dealer for thinking that you are out to get his coins! For sure, the dealer would have had past experiences along this line. You know it is very easy to palm coins and drop them into your purse, bag, or pockets and not get noticed at all. So, stop giving the dealer a reason to suspect that you are out to pocket his coins. Always show your hands palms up and if you must take out something from your purse or pocket, tell the dealer what you are about to do. If you have been picking up coins (remember to hold them by the edge) you want to buy and must move to give way to other customers, let the dealer hold the coins for you. Never for a moment (this is essential for your survival in your first coin show or any subsequent show for that matter) step away from the dealer's table with coins you haven't paid yet. You do not want the dealer to think you are stealing his coins. People have been thrown out of coin shows this way. D. You take great pride in your growing coin collection, and you want to showcase it to the world. There are various ways to display your coins, such as using display cases, boxes, picture frames, folders, or presentation binders. You can also use a bookcase or cabinet to exhibit your collection at home, either as a permanent display or for special occasions. The key is to make it as visually appealing as possible.

If you plan to sell your collection in the future, consider using attractive leather or vinyl coin albums or sleeves to showcase your American coins. Custom albums for displaying American dimes, pennies, and nickels are available in online stores. For your most treasured coins, display them in a wooden cabinet with velvet linings.

If you want to prepare your coins for a coin show or exhibit, follow the lead of many collectors by placing them inside a coin collecting album designed to display coins in all their splendor. These albums are meant to be seen and admired, not hidden away in a drawer somewhere. By displaying your coins in a collecting album, you can draw attention to their beauty and intricate details, captivating anyone who sets eyes on them.

CHAPTER 2

THE PERFECT TIME TO SELL COINS

When is the best time to sell your coins?

This may seem silly to ask a mint piece authority, but time does make a difference. There are instances when a coin collector wakes up in the early morning hours and decides to sell his prized collection of coins. Sometimes, a collector must give up his mint piece collections for personal reasons, and selling his prized coins might be the most difficult aspect of the process. This happens in the life of a mint piece authority for various reasons. Mint piece collectors sell their currency for various reasons, and there is also mint piece authority that sells their wares. It is their choice to sell coins, and they may do so to generate funds to purchase other coins they prefer. A few officials travel in search of a mint piece they require, and while doing so, they may encounter currencies that are not suitable for their collection; yet, they obtain them regardless. When they return, they sell the coins and use the money to buy the coins they're looking for.

Some coin collectors collect coins not just as a hobby but as a source of income. They make a living by selling the coins they acquire. These collectors may sell the coins to various entities at a higher price than their face value, particularly if the coins are limited editions or rare.

On the other hand, a few collectors sell their coins owing to various factors. They may sell coins for a variety of reasons. Authorities occasionally choose to "part with" their collection since they have no other option but to sell their coins. This is the most difficult situation for mint piece collectors since they frequently value their currencies and, as one might anticipate, have no want to part with them - the currencies may be souvenirs or have a nostalgic value to the authority.

When a collector decides to sell his coins, he should assess whether this is the best time.

Is the authority willing to hand over his money?

Is the currency now more expensive than before?

Will it go smoothly, and will he make money by selling his coins?

These aspects should be kept in mind at all times.

Several options are available for determining where a mint piece collector could sell his coins. He might have to bargain for the coins. Many people are now leaning toward making their assets accessible for purchase, which isn't limited to mint piece collections.

Due to offering forms in swaps, there is also a greater chance of selling the coin at a higher price. Purchasers may offer a higher price, especially if the sold coin is of exceptional quality and worth. A coin collector may also need to create a website to market the coins he wants to sell. The Internet is the most convenient way to search for coins for coin collectors. Furthermore, posting the coin on the Internet will make selling it much easier. The authority may create his website and post photographs of his coins and brief descriptions. He should also keep track of how much he is willing to sell them.

There are also other options: the merchant may need to conduct a vendor-to-seller trade. He can properly sell his coins to coin dealers. At that point, the sellers can sell the coins they purchased to other vendors.

It is critical to consider costs while comparing one seller to another, as there is always the possibility that one dealer will pay a higher price for the coins than other sellers. It's smart to start by looking for vendors and then deciding which ones you need to handle.

It is also recommended that coin collectors who wish to sell their coins use a coin reviewing service. It is signed to prevent the dealer from becoming a washout when selling his coins. By utilizing an evaluating service, the dealer will be able to set a value based on the appraisal produced by the evaluating service, which will determine the true value of the coins. Once a currency authority has decided to sell its coins, it should not improve them. If they do, the value of the coins will plummet.

CHAPTER 3

DEFECTIVE & COUNTERFEIT COINS

Counterfeit and altered coins are more than a bother; they are fraudulent coins that detract from the hobby of coin collecting. They betray our faith in the coins and one another, and they detract from the enjoyment of the pastime.

Customers lose tens of thousands of dollars every year when they unwittingly buy fake or altered coins. Each day, someone within the United States purchases a counterfeit coin without realizing it. Unfortunately, the person who sold the coin is often unaware that it is a fake or tampered with coin. Federal legislation exists that makes it illegal to duplicate or alter a genuine coin to improve its numismatic value. However, this does not deter the lowlife criminals who continue to produce thousands of counterfeit and altered coins each year. Many websites purchase counterfeit coins of almost any denomination ever issued by the United States Mint. Most of these sites are located in Asia, where copyrights, patents, and trademarks are routinely ignored and infringed. Although the central government is aware of the situation, there are not many actions to deter violators. It is your responsibility to understand the coin you purchase and preserve your investment.

WHAT IS A FORGERY COIN?

What is a coin that has been tampered with?

A fake coin is made to look like a real coin. An ordinary coin that has been altered by adding and removing metal to imitate a scarce or expensive numismatic coin is known as an altered coin. Over time, crooks have improved their ability to create counterfeit coins. The manufacturing procedures utilized to manufacture the fake coins have evolved as technology has advanced. In one situation I'm aware of, counterfeit coins are minted the same way as genuine ones.

The counterfeiters are daring enough, or stupid enough, to photograph their minting operation and post it on the internet. The issue isn't confined to high-value numismatic coins. Any coin with a considerable quality has been forged. Coins of the United States of America, $1 American Silver Eagle bullion coins, have recently been discovered to be counterfeited.

COPY   **REAL**

They were of such excellent quality that even coin experts were duped when they first saw them. Counterfeiters have targeted coins ranging from a dime to a $20 Double Eagle gold coin. So, how can you safeguard yourself, your money, and your pastime?

Fortunately, counterfeit coin detection technologies are readily available and simple to use. The best tools to utilize are, for the most part, your eyes and your brain.

3.1 How to Spot Fake and Alternate Coins?

1. If the offer appears to be too good or to be true:

In the realm of coins, most valuable coins will sell for close to their retail value. The only exclusions are coins that the seller does not know about. That will be rare, though, although most individuals know how to calculate the worth of a coin. Coins offered for a few cents on the dollar should be avoided. If you're presented with a rare coin that you know is worth thousands of dollars, but the seller wants a few dollars for it, it's most likely a fake. Any coin purchased from a seller who does not provide a suitable return policy should be avoided. Most reputable dealers have a policy that permits you to return a coin after inspecting it and discovering flaws.

2. BE FAMILIAR WITH THE COIN YOU'RE INTRIGUED BY:

Before you purchase a high-value coin, please do some research on it? Look for photos of authentic coins and study both the obverse and reverse sides. Learn everything there is to know about the coin, including its current value. Compare the coin to recognized genuine coins or high-resolution images of the coin.

A Morgan silver dollar was once handed to me for purchase by a friend's acquaintance. It was a stunning coin in mint condition! So why didn't I go out and buy it? It was a forgery. The Branch Mint did not produce any Morgan dollars, and the coin did not exist. That isn't the first time I've seen similar fake coins. That's why it's crucial to understand everything there is to know about the coin you're purchasing. This is particularly true with tampered coins.

The term "altered coins" refers to coins that look like something they are not. The Mercury Dime from 1916-D is a great example. A plain Philadelphia struck dime with no mint stamp is given a "D" mintmark by coin doctors. A magnification examination of the coin reveals the deception.

3. COINS WITH A CERTIFICATE OF AUTHENTICITY:

When buying high-value coins, consider acquiring only coins certified by one of the three leading third-party grading firms, PCGS, NGC, or ANACS. Any coins that a different firm has encapsulated are dubious. PCGS, NGC, and ANACS determine whether a coin is genuine. Always double-check that the slabbed coin you're interested in is the same coin that PCGS, NGC, or ANACS have sealed.

Slabs from these grading companies have been proven to be fakes. Each of the three companies listed above has an online database with photographs of the validated coins. Check the coin you wish to buy against that internet database to ensure it's the same one.

3.2 HOW TO SUSPECT COUNTERFEIT COINS ARE PUT TO THE TEST:

1. Use a powerful magnet to examine the coin. The United States Mint has created only one coin that will be pulled to a magnet. The 1943 Lincoln Cent was made of steel planchets, and China produced most counterfeit coins using planchets made of iron. If any US-minted coin you test is even marginally attracted to the magnet, it's a fake. Determine the weight of the coin. The weight of all coins produced by the United States Mint is known and will only vary by roughly 1%. Make sure you choose a scale that measures tenths of grams. Diet scales are insufficiently accurate. Place the coin on the scale and check its weight to the coin's stated weight. Don't buy it if it varies by 1% above or below that weight.

3. Calculate the value of the coin. Measure the coin's diameter with a small-scale caliper. The diameter of every coin struck in the United States is known. In most circumstances, if the measurement fluctuates by more than 1%, the coin is counterfeit.

4. Look at the coin's surfaces. Examine the coin using an 8X-10X magnifying. If the coin appears lumpy or bubbling, it may be a fake. Poured metals are commonly used to create coins with these indicators. Examine the coin's edge for traces of pouring, such as seams in the metal. All U.S. coins with a denomination greater than 5 cents have reeded edges. If the reeds are uneven or missing, the coin is likely fake.

5. Keep a list of U.S. coins handy. The Redbook U.S. Coin reference series is one of my favorites. They're in almost every coin shop I've ever visited. Come in and meet the dealer, browse his coin collection, and pick up the most recent copy. The weight and diameter of each coin issued by the United States Mint are shown.

Get one, put it on your desk, and consult it whenever you have a coin-related question. When purchasing high-value items, there will always be hazards. That applies to everything. There are counterfeits of almost any popular product you can think of in the marketplace. Guitars, blenders, trousers, purses, and even automobiles have been counterfeited.

Before you hand over your cash, make sure you know what you're getting. This tutorial won't detect every fake or changed coin, and it will find the obvious flaws. Counterfeiters have been improving their malicious work. Well-made fake coins have duped even professionals in the subject. You can reduce your risk by learning about your currencies and testing the coins you're considering buying. You will come across counterfeit coins and coins that have been made to look like something they are not at some time throughout your coin collecting career. Be ready. It is your most effective defense.

CHAPTER 4

SOME USEFUL TIPS

4.1 TIPS FOR COIN COLLECTION:

Before you begin, I'd want to offer some coin collecting advice based on what I've learned so far. Coin collecting can be a highly gratifying hobby, and perhaps this guide will help you become a better collector.

HAVE PATIENCE:

Take some time to educate yourself before diving in and buying MS-70, Capped-Bust Dimes. Begin by looking at various coins to see what you prefer, such as artistic, historical, or quality coins. Read some actual works on coin collecting then grading, and maintenance.

SPECIALIZE:

After casting an extensive net, it's time to narrow your attention and specialized in a specific collection of coins. Consider what fascinates you: British sovereigns, Lincoln pennies, or 1800 silver quarters, for example. The more you specialized, the easier it will be to understand rating and value, or the less likely you will be taken advantage of. This will create coin collecting a whole lot more fun!

SET OBJECTIVES:

Setting goals can be significant as you focus on particular coin sets, you want to pursue.

When you finish 'your collection,' it is advantageous, and almost everyone wants to have that perfect collection to exhibition. Coins Collection will be much more enjoyable if you have defined goals in mind.

SEEK PROFESSIONAL ASSISTANCE:

Don't be reluctant to ask for help when starting, especially if you need to grade a coin. Learning from an elder collector might also provide helpful guidance.

Visit local dealers and coin stores regularly and get to know them by name

SPEAK RIGHT LANGUAGE:

Another helpful approach is to learn the terminology used by numismatists when conversing a coin. Brockage, bag markings and business strikes are all collecting coin phrases that you should be familiar with before approaching a dealer/seller or attending your first coin exhibition. You'll discover that many merchants are humble, accommodating, and courteous. The PCGS website includes a helpful dictionary of collecting jargon. You should be familiar with the composition of a coin.

4.2 Tips for Buying Coins

Collecting coin is a skill that may be learned through time. The important thing to recall is that you are doing it for the correct reasons; it is worthwhile to pursue, if it is a craze or passion. Collecting coins just for revenue may be effective in the short term, but it is rarely sufficient in the long-term. A lot of people who have attempted it for that motive have failed because they have lost concentration.

Fruitful coin collectors devote a significant amount of effort to learning everything there is to know about numismatics. Newsletters, magazines, and brokers who can provide information and news as it happens are good sources of information. A person could move rapidly before new collectors who desire the same thing receive the information by exploiting the resources. If an individual attempts to gather without first learning the fundamentals, he will fail miserably. Knowing how to grade coins can also assist a collector in determining the true value of their collection. This information will be useful if the owner selects to exchange for something of higher value or help prevent scams and squandering money on something of low value. Always be on the lookout! Because a coin collection might take years to complete, one of the virtues that coin collecting can teach is patience.

Several of the world's most well-known collectors have waited many years to reap the benefits. It's critical to learn to think like a coin collector. Too much excitement is bad because a collector may be enticed to acquire or exchange the incorrect coin, which could be pricey. Even if the information originated from a trusted source, think twice before using it.

Collecting coin can be difficult, mainly for those just getting started. A person's budget is unlikely to allow him to purchase articles worth more than $10,000, so it's best to start a small and investigate the market for 3 to 6 months before pursuing largest prizes.

Collecting coin is parallel to sports, it took time to master and that immediate and longstanding goals must be demonstrated. The person could join the ranks of different other expert coin collectors by following the guidelines and employing common sense.

BOOK 6 – MOST VALUABLE COINS

INTRODUCTION

In a world where spare change often goes unnoticed, a hidden treasure trove of valuable coins is waiting to be discovered. Welcome to "15 Common Coins Worth Big Money That Could Be in Your Pocket Change," where we embark on a journey to uncover the unexpected riches hiding in plain sight.

Have you ever thought that the coins jingling in your pocket could hold more value than their face value suggests? Imagine the thrill of finding a coin worth thousands of dollars among the familiar jumble of coins you encounter every day. This mini ebook is your guide to identifying those diamonds in the rough – coins that might look ordinary but hold extraordinary worth.

While the term "pocket change" might conjure images of insignificant coins, you're about to discover that appearances can be deceiving. These common coins have stories to tell, and their tales are laced with value far beyond what you'd expect. From simple misstrikes to mint errors, these coins have become numismatic treasures, sought after by collectors and enthusiasts around the world.

As we dive into the pages ahead, you'll learn to identify the key attributes that set these coins apart. Some coins bear unique markings or doubling, while others were minted on unexpected materials or with intriguing errors. We'll cover coins from various eras and denominations, each with its own tale of rarity and intrigue.

So, whether you're a seasoned numismatist seeking new discoveries or someone who's never thought twice about the coins in your pocket, this mini ebook promises to open your eyes to a world of hidden wealth. Join us as we explore the fascinating stories and remarkable value behind these 15 common coins that could be lurking right under your fingertips. Let's dive in and start our journey of uncovering the valuable secrets hidden within the realm of pocket change.

CHAPTER 1: FINDING VALUABLE COINS: LET'S START THE COUNTDOWN

Let's dive into something exciting – finding out which coins hiding in your pockets could be worth more than you think. These aren't just regular coins; they have unique stories that make them extra valuable. Prepare for surprises as we count down the most valuable coins you might have without knowing it.

Starting at Number 10: The Funny-Looking Quarter - A Quirk That Makes It Valuable.

Imagine reaching into your pocket and pulling out a coin that doesn't look like the rest. That's the story behind the 1999 Philadelphia Mint Connecticut Broad Struck Quarter. What makes this coin special isn't just its age or the picture on it – it's the mistake that happened when it was made.

You see when coins are made, they go through a minting process where metal is pressed to create the design. But sometimes, things don't go exactly as planned. In the case of these quarters, something went a little wonky during the pressing, causing them to be "broad-struck." This means they weren't lined up perfectly on the minting press, leading to a design that's a bit different from the usual.

The result? Quarters that have a unique appearance. The edges might be slightly different, the design might be slightly off-center, or other small quirks could make these coins stand out from the crowd. And it's these imperfections that make them valuable to collectors.

So, why would someone want a coin that's not perfectly made? Well, the world of coin collecting is full of enthusiasts who love the stories behind each coin. These funny-looking quarters are like little pieces of history that tell a tale of a moment when the minting process didn't go as planned.

But wait, there's more! The value of these coins adds an exciting twist. If you happen to stumble upon one of these 1999 Philadelphia Mint Connecticut Broad Struck Quarters, you could be holding a coin that's worth $25. That's a big leap from the 25 cents it was originally meant to be worth!

You might be wondering, "Why would someone pay so much for a coin that's not perfect?" Well, it's all about rarity and uniqueness. Collectors are willing to pay a premium for coins that have stories to tell – coins that stand out from the ordinary. And when you hold one of these funny-looking quarters, you're not just holding a piece of currency; you're holding a piece of history, a moment frozen in time when things didn't quite go according to plan.

So, the next time you're sorting through your change or peering into your coin jar, keep an eye out for that one quarter that looks a little different. It might just be one of those 1999 Philadelphia Mint Connecticut Broad Struck Quarters, and you could be holding a treasure that's worth far more than you ever imagined.

NUMBER 9: THE COIN WITH A GREASE PROBLEM - THE TALE BEHIND "IN GOD WE RUST"

Picture this: a coin that's supposed to say "In God We Trust," but instead, it proudly displays the phrase "In God We Rust." Yes, you read that right –

rust! But before you imagine a bunch of rusty coins, let's dive into the fascinating story behind the 2005 Philadelphia Mint Kansas State Quarter.

Coins are like little pieces of art, and making them is a delicate dance of precision. When putting words on coins, a metal punch with letters is used to create the design. But what happens when the metal punch isn't as clean as it should be? This is where the greasy mistake comes into play.

In the case of the 2005 Kansas State Quarter, there was a tiny but crucial detail: a piece of the letter "T" on the metal punch was clogged with grease. As a result, when the coin was being made, that grease prevented the "T" from properly stamping onto the coin. And just like that, "Trust" turned into "Rust."

You might be wondering how something like this slipped through the cracks. Well, coins are made in large quantities, and errors can sometimes go unnoticed until they're in the hands of the public. Imagine the surprise of the people who first noticed the typo on these coins!

But here's the fun part: mistakes like these, known as minting errors, often make coins even more interesting to collectors. They tell a story of the human element behind the creation of coins – the little accidents that can turn an ordinary piece of currency into something truly unique.

Now, let's talk about value. You might think that a coin with a mistake like "In God We Rust" would be worth next to nothing, right? Wrong! Because these coins are rare and have a quirky story, collectors are eager to have them in their collections. If you have one of these coins lying around – maybe in a jar or mixed in with your spare change – you could be holding a coin worth $100.

Yes, that's right – a coin with a greasy mishap could make you smile when you realize it's worth more than its face value. It's a reminder that sometimes mistakes make things more interesting, and that a tiny typo can turn a coin into a conversation starter.

So, next time you're looking at your coins, keep an eye out for the 2005 Philadelphia Mint Kansas State Quarter with the "In God We Rust" variation. It's a piece of coin history that shows even the smallest mistakes can turn into something pretty cool. Who knew a little grease could add some value and excitement to your spare change?

NUMBER 8: THE DOUBLE-EARED PENNY - THE UNINTENDED RARITY

Abraham Lincoln is a name that echoes throughout history as one of America's most famous presidents. But did you know Lincoln's portrait has a surprising secret in the world of coins? In 1997, something unexpected happened while making coins that turned Lincoln into a man with not one, but two earlobes! Let's unravel the tale behind this quirky mistake and its value.

First, picture Abraham Lincoln. Tall and towering at 6 feet 4 inches, he was quite a presence. Now, imagine a coin bearing his image, showcasing a unique trait that even history books might not mention – the presence of double earlobes.

In the coin-making process, an image of Lincoln is carefully engraved onto a metal die. This die is then used to create the design on the coin. But in 1997, the process took an unexpected twist. Somehow, the engravers accidentally gave Lincoln two earlobes on the coin instead of the usual one.

This seemingly simple mistake turned out to be a numismatic gem. It's the kind of unexpected surprise that collectors treasure. Instead of a typical, picture-perfect portrayal, this coin carries a human touch, a reminder that even the most famous figures in history aren't immune to the occasional quirky error.

Now, let's talk value. You might think a coin with a simple mistake wouldn't be worth much, but you'd be surprised. Collectors, always looking for something different, find these coins fascinating. If you happen to be the lucky owner of a 1997 Lincoln penny with double earlobes, you could be looking at an extra $250 in your pocket.

Imagine that – a small, seemingly ordinary coin could turn out to be a little treasure worth far more than its face value. It's not about the metal; it's about the story. The story of a moment in time when a minting error made a president look a bit different, a story that's now etched into that very coin.

So, the next time you're glancing at your pocket change, take a closer look at the 1997 Lincoln pennies. If you spot one with double earlobes, you might just be holding a piece of history and a small windfall – a delightful reminder that even in the world of coins, sometimes mistakes can lead to extraordinary discoveries.

NUMBER 7: THE DIME WITH NO MARK: A HIDDEN AMUSEMENT

Coins tell stories about their origins with their unique marks and designs. But in 1982, something unusual happened in the coin-making world – a bunch of dimes were released into the wild without the marks that usually indicate where they were made. This tiny omission turned these dimes into intriguing pieces of numismatic history, especially when they found their way to an unexpected destination.

You might wonder, what are these marks, and why are they important? Well, those little letters on coins – like "P" for Philadelphia, "D" for Denver, and "S" for San Francisco – tell us where the coins were minted. They're like little stamps of origin that add to the coin's story.

But in 1982, the marks were mysteriously missing from some dimes. Imagine coins without their usual identity! These "markless" dimes raised eyebrows and questions among collectors and enthusiasts. It's like a puzzle – how did this happen? Was it a mistake, or was there a purpose behind it?

The mystery deepens with a fun twist. Many of these markless dimes ended up circulating at Cedar Point Amusement Park in Sandusky, Ohio. Picture this: you're enjoying a day at the amusement park, and as you spend your coins on rides and treats, you might unknowingly come across one of these unique dimes.

Now, let's talk value. You might think that coins without their marks wouldn't be worth much, but that's where the collector's interest comes in. These markless dimes have become little treasures that collectors want to have. If you're lucky enough to find one in your pocket change or hidden in a jar of coins, you could be holding something worth around $300.

Isn't that a fun surprise? A little markless dime traveling through time and landing at an amusement park could turn into a small windfall. The universe is giving you a little bonus for being part of this fascinating coin story.

So, the next time you're emptying your pockets or checking your coin jar, watch for those 1982 dimes that might be missing their marks. You never know – you could be holding a piece of history that's worth more than its face value. And think, the value of that coin could be like a free pass to your little amusement park of discovery!

Number 6: The Speared Bison Nickel - a Scratch That Sparked Value

Imagine a nickel that tells a story through its design – a story of a bison that looks like it got poked by a spear. But here's the fascinating part: it's not an intentional design choice; it's a scratch during the coin-making process.

Welcome to the intriguing world of the 2005 Speared Bison Jefferson Nickel, a coin that turned an accident into something incredibly valuable.

Let's dive into the image on this nickel. The bison, a majestic symbol of the American West, appears like a spear has gone right through its side. It's a striking visual, one that sparks curiosity and wonder. But believe it or not, this isn't an artistic choice made by the coin's creators; it's the result of a deep scratch on the metal die used to make the coin.

Creating coins involves pressing metal to transfer the design onto the coin's surface. Sometimes, during this intricate process, things can go slightly awry. In the case of the Speared Bison Nickel, a scratch occurred on the die, leaving its mark on the coins it produced.

Now, let's talk value. You might think that a scratch would devalue a coin, but here's where the coin-collecting world turns interesting. Collectors are drawn to coins with unique and unusual features – the kind of features that tell a story. The accidental scratch on the Speared Bison Nickel turned it into a conversation starter and a sought-after piece among collectors.

In fact, one of these nickels sold for more than a thousand dollars. That's right – a coin with a scratch, or rather, a "spear," became a valuable treasure for someone who saw beyond the imperfection to the story it told.

So, if you're ever going through your coins and happen upon a 2005 Speared Bison Jefferson Nickel, take a moment to appreciate the accident that turned it into a piece of art with a tale. That seemingly minor scratch transformed a regular coin into something extraordinary, reminding us that sometimes, unexpected twists can add value and intrigue to the most unexpected places. Who knew a scratch could make a nickel a hidden treasure waiting to be discovered?

NUMBER 5: THE LEAFY QUARTER: UNVEILING NATURE'S SECRET ON THE 2004 WISCONSIN STATE QUARTER

Imagine holding a quarter with the usual design and a little surprise – an extra leaf. This is the story of the 2004 Wisconsin State Quarter, a coin that carries a hidden detail like a wink from the creators. Let's uncover the mystery behind this leafy addition and explore how it turned some ordinary quarters into something unexpectedly valuable.

The 2004 Wisconsin State Quarter features a depiction of a cow, a wheel of cheese, and an ear of corn – all symbols of the state's agricultural heritage. But in the world of coin collecting, a few of these quarters have a little extra – an additional leaf on the ear of corn. It's like a secret message, a small twist that makes these coins stand out.

So, how did this extra leaf end up on the coin? Well, it's believed to be the result of a deliberate action taken by someone in the minting process. Perhaps a mint worker decided to add a little creative touch, or it was a way to leave a personal mark on the coins they were producing. Whatever the reason, it transformed these quarters into tiny treasures with a unique story.

Now, let's talk value. You might think that a simple extra leaf wouldn't make a big difference, but in coin collecting, uniqueness and rarity are key factors. Because only a few of these quarters have the extra leaf, they've become sought-after by collectors who appreciate the novelty and intrigue of these hidden details.

Interestingly, a significant number of these extra-leaf quarters were found in Tucson, Arizona. These discoveries added to the mystery and charm surrounding these coins. Combining the unique variation and the connection to a specific place has given these quarters added value.

If you are the lucky owner of one of these 2004 Wisconsin State Quarters with the extra leaf, you could be holding something worth up to $1,499.

Yes, that's right – a simple quarter with an extra leaf could turn out to be a small windfall, proving that sometimes, even the tiniest of details can lead to unexpected treasure.

So, the next time you're sorting through your change or checking your coin jar, keep an eye out for those extra-leaf quarters. You never know – you might have a hidden gem in your possession, a quarter that's worth far more than its face value. It's a reminder that even in the world of coins, a little twist of nature's artistry can make all the difference.

NUMBER 4: THE COIN THAT MIRRORS ITSELF - THE DOUBLE DIE LINCOLN PENNY

Imagine a coin that appears to be looking at itself in a mirror –the tale of the 1955 Double Die Lincoln Penny. This coin carries a mistake that turned it into a numismatic wonder, capturing a moment when the minting process took an unexpected twist. Let's delve into the story of this double-impression coin and how it transformed into something incredibly valuable.

With its portrait of Abraham Lincoln, the Lincoln penny is a familiar face in the world of coins. But in 1955, something extraordinary happened – a batch of pennies got stamped twice, creating a unique effect that echoes the design. It's like a coin that decided to make a double appearance.

So, how did this happen? When creating coins, metal dies are used to transfer the design onto the coin's surface. In the case of the 1955 Double Die Lincoln Penny, a misalignment or glitch caused the design to be imprinted twice, slightly offset from each other. This created a captivating visual effect, making it look like the coin's features were duplicated.

Now, let's talk value. You might wonder why a coin with what seems like a mistake would be worth anything. But in coin collecting, rarity and uniqueness are highly prized. These coins with the double impression are like little pieces of history, capturing a moment when the minting process went slightly off track.

Collectors are intrigued by coins that tell stories, and the 1955 Double Die Lincoln Penny is a story that's etched right onto the coin itself. Because these coins are rare and sought-after, their value has climbed over the years.

If you're one of the fortunate individuals who happen to possess a 1955 Double Die Lincoln Penny, you could be holding something worth up to $3,000. Yes, you read that right – a small, seemingly ordinary penny could turn into a small fortune, reminding us that even the smallest of mistakes can lead to extraordinary outcomes.

So, the next time you're sifting through your coins or examining your coin collection, keep an eye out for that penny that seems to be looking back at you. It might just be one of these rare and valuable coins, a tiny artifact that tells a tale of a double impression and a hefty value. It's a testament to the fact that even in the world of coins, sometimes a unique twist can turn a common item into an unexpected treasure.

Number 3: The Close "AM" Penny - A Peculiar Pairing of Letters Worth Thousands

Imagine a penny where the letters seem huddled up, almost as if they're close friends. This is the fascinating story of the 1992 Close "AM" Penny, a coin that stands out due to an unusual and rare feature on its reverse side. Let's delve into the details of this curious penny and explore why its unique letter arrangement makes it so valuable.

You might not pay much attention to the letters when you look at a penny. But in 1992, something out of the ordinary happened. On the reverse side of the penny, the letters "A" and "M" in the inscription "United States of

America" are surprisingly close together. It's as if they decided to cozy up for a conversation.

So, how did this happen? The process of creating coin dies involves precision, but sometimes, variations occur. In the case of the 1992 Close "AM" Penny, a slight misalignment or anomaly during the die-making process led to the letters "A" and "M" being placed closer than usual. This minuscule alteration turned an ordinary penny into a rare find.

Now, let's talk value. Rarity is a significant factor in coin collecting, and the 1992 Close "AM" Penny is a prime example. Due to the limited number of pennies with this specific variation, collectors eagerly seek them out. The uniqueness of the coin's letter arrangement adds to its allure.

Because of its rarity and intrigue, the 1992 Close "AM" Penny has become a coin of substantial value. In fact, if you happen to possess one of these close-lettered pennies, you could be holding something worth over $24,000. Yes, that's right – a simple penny with a subtle alteration could turn into a small fortune.

So, the next time you're sorting through your coins or exploring your collection, take a closer look at those 1992 pennies. If you spot one where the "A" and "M" appear to be close companions, you might be holding a far more valuable treasure than its face value. It's a reminder that even the tiniest of details can significantly impact an ordinary coin into a rare and sought-after artifact in the world of numismatics.

NUMBER 2: THE PENNY THAT PIQUED THE FBI'S CURIOSITY – THE INTRIGUING TALE OF THE 1969 S DOUBLE DIE REVERSE PENNY

Imagine a penny that's so extraordinary, it caught the attention of none other than the FBI. This is the captivating story of the 1969 S Lincoln Penny with Double Die Reverse, a coin that made waves due to its remarkable appearance. Let's delve into the fascinating journey of this penny and discover why its uniqueness led to an unexpected encounter with the FBI.

In 1969, something astonishing happened during the minting process of a batch of pennies. The design on the coin's reverse side appeared to be doubled – as if it had been stamped twice, slightly offset. This gave the penny a distinctive and almost surreal appearance, a trait that collectors immediately found intriguing.

Now, here's where things get interesting. The uniqueness of the 1969 S Double Die Reverse Penny was so striking that even the Federal Bureau of Investigation (FBI) took notice. They suspected these coins were counterfeits because they looked, unlike any other pennies in circulation. The FBI's involvement turned this coin into an unexpected protagonist in numismatics.

However, further investigation revealed that these pennies were legitimate and not counterfeit. They resulted from a fascinating anomaly in the minting process, one that created a coin with a double impression on its reverse side. This made the 1969 S Double Die Reverse Penny an accidental masterpiece, capturing a moment when the coin-making process took an unexpected turn.

Now, let's talk value. The rarity of this particular penny has made it a highly sought-after item among collectors. The coin's appearance, combined with its connection to the FBI, adds to its allure. One of these pennies was sold for more than $100,000 – a staggering sum that reflects the coin's significance in numismatics.

Just think about it – a simple penny that fooled the FBI and became a valuable treasure for a lucky collector. It's a testament to the notion that even the most unexpected items can hold remarkable stories and surprising worth.

So, the next time you come across a 1969 S Double Die Reverse Penny, take a moment to appreciate its journey – from catching the eye of the FBI to becoming a sought-after gem among collectors. It's a small reminder that a unique twist of fate can elevate an ordinary coin to a position of extraordinary value and intrigue in the realm of coins.

THE ULTIMATE COIN CHAMPION: THE ASTONISHING TALE OF THE 1943 COPPER PENNY

Ladies and gentlemen, the moment has arrived – presenting the reigning champion of coins, the 1943 Copper Penny. Brace yourselves for a story that combines history, rarity, and a touch of accidental magic. This penny's narrative is extraordinary in a world where coins tell tales.

Travel back to the year 1943, a time when the intensity of war gripped the world. In an effort to contribute to the war effort, the majority of pennies produced during that time were made of steel, a departure from the traditional copper composition. However, as fate would have it, some intriguing mistakes occurred in the minting process, giving birth to a handful of copper pennies, defying the norm.

These accidental copper pennies hold remarkable significance. Their existence is a testament to the unpredictability of coin production, a glimpse into a time when even the most meticulous processes could be disrupted. A handful of these unique coins slipped through the cracks of a wartime economy dominated by steel, turning into hidden gems that tell a tale of unexpected variation.

Now, let's talk value. The rarity of the 1943 Copper Penny is what sets it apart as the ultimate treasure among coin collectors. While most people might not give a second thought to a penny, the allure of this exceptional copper variant has led to staggering numbers. One of these pennies was sold for an astonishing $1,700,000, a figure reflecting the coin's rarity and significance in the world of numismatics.

Imagine holding a penny worth more than most people can dream of in your hand. The 1943 Copper Penny is a testament to the idea that value can be found in the most unexpected places. It's a shining example of how historical context, rarity, and unique circumstances can elevate a simple object into a symbol of immense worth.

So, if you happen to stumble upon a 1943 Copper Penny, know that you're holding a piece of history that's truly one of a kind. It's a reminder that even in the smallest of denominations, incredible stories can unfold, and unexpected riches can be found. The 1943 Copper Penny has proven itself as the ultimate coin champion, showcasing that sometimes, even a penny can become a ticket to an extraordinary journey of discovery and value.

Conclusion

And thus, our journey through the world of hidden treasures ends. As we conclude our countdown of coins that could be silently residing in your pockets, purses, or coin jars, we're left with a profound realization: the ordinary can often hide the extraordinary. Who would have thought that the loose change we often overlook could hold the potential to unlock unexpected riches?

Our journey has peeled back the layers of everyday coins, revealing stories of mistakes that turned into masterpieces, quirky designs that transformed into sought-after artifacts, and accidental anomalies that led to extraordinary values. Each coin on our countdown has shown us that the world of numismatics is brimming with surprises, waiting to be uncovered by those with a keen eye and a touch of luck.

So, as you go about your days, remember that the world of coin collecting isn't just for experts or enthusiasts – it's for everyone. Every coin you encounter has the potential to be a hidden gem, a tiny window into history, and a piece of artistry that holds more value than meets the eye.

Keep your eyes open and your curiosity alive. The 1999 Philadelphia Mint Connecticut Broad Struck Quarter, the 2005 Philadelphia Mint Kansas State Quarter with its "In God We Rust" message, the 1992 Close "AM" Penny, the 1969 S Double Die Reverse Penny that caught the FBI's attention, and the awe-inspiring 1943 Copper Penny – these coins are proof that the world of coins is a treasure trove waiting to be explored.

As you handle your change or admire your coin collection, remember that the stories behind these coins are as valuable as the coins themselves. They remind us that every coin has a tale to tell, a history to unfold, and a value beyond its face.

So, keep the spirit of discovery alive, whether you're a seasoned collector or someone who's just starting to delve into the world of coins. Uncovering these hidden treasures doesn't end with this countdown; it's a lifelong adventure that promises surprises, insights, and a deeper appreciation for the everyday items that have the power to tell extraordinary stories.

Who knew the coins in our pockets could hold such a wealth of secrets? Indeed, every coin is a potential treasure waiting to be discovered. So, keep your eyes open, for who knows what hidden riches may lurk in your pockets and coin jars.

Chapter 2: Introduction to Valuable Coins

Coins are more than mere currency; they're windows into history, culture, and, sometimes, immense value. This chapter serves as your gateway into the world of valuable coins hiding within everyday pocket change. From viewing coins as mundane tokens to recognizing them as potential treasures, prepare to shift your perspective.

In our daily routines, we often overlook the coins we handle – the quarters we toss into vending machines, the pennies that collect at the bottom of our bags, and the dimes that accumulate in our pockets. But what if some of these coins held the potential to change our financial fortunes?

The concept of valuable coins hiding in plain sight is more than a mere possibility – it's a reality. These unassuming bits of metal, minted with precision and care, can sometimes hold rare attributes that elevate their worth far beyond what their nominal value suggests. The thrill of stumbling upon such a coin, whether in pocket change, coin rolls, or even a bank teller's tray, is akin to finding a hidden gem in a sea of ordinary stones.

This chapter sets the stage for the exciting journey ahead by opening your eyes to the vast potential in your everyday interactions with coins. It encourages you to ask questions, explore possibilities, and look beyond the surface to uncover the hidden stories and values embedded within these seemingly mundane objects.

As you read on, remember that the world of numismatics is rich with history, curiosity, and speculation. It's a space where meticulous research and a keen eye can yield unexpected dividends. By the time you finish this chapter, you'll be primed to delve deeper into the world of valuable coins, armed with the knowledge needed to embark on a rewarding treasure hunt within your own pocket change.

Are you ready to unveil the true potential of coins and unlock their hidden worth? Let's continue our journey and discover the first set of coins that could be hiding exceptional value right under your nose.

CHAPTER 3: UNVEILING THE HIDDEN TREASURES

Every coin has a story, a journey from the mint to your pocket, from generation to generation. Within this narrative lies the potential for extraordinary discoveries – coins that stand out for their historical significance and hidden value. In this chapter, we delve into the concept of valuable coins hiding in plain sight and the excitement of uncovering these hidden treasures.

Coins are an integral part of daily life. We use them to make purchases, as well as symbols of commemoration and heritage. However, their worth doesn't stop at their face value. Hidden within the vast sea of coins in circulation are pieces with attributes that elevate them to collector's items, rarities that are highly sought after in the numismatic community.

Imagine sifting through a handful of coins and discovering that one holds a value far beyond what you could have imagined. It's a thrilling prospect – a reminder that there's more to the everyday objects around us than meets the eye. These discoveries are not reserved for experts; they're accessible to anyone willing to learn, observe, and be curious.

Uncovering valuable coins begins with understanding that rarity and value can often be found in unexpected places. A coin with a slight variation, a minting error, or a unique historical context can make all the difference. This chapter prepares you to shift your perspective, encouraging you to scrutinize the coins you encounter and consider the possibility that something exceptional might be hiding among them.

While these treasures may be common in terms of circulation, their numismatic value makes them far from ordinary. Learning to recognize these attributes and differentiate them from their more common counterparts is an art that can be cultivated with time and practice. This chapter sets the stage for your exploration, urging you to adopt a collector's mindset and embark on a journey of discovery.

As we wrap up this chapter, consider the coins you've encountered daily. What if some of those seemingly unremarkable pieces held a story that could be worth more than you ever thought? In the coming chapters, we'll dive into specific coins that have transformed from commonplace to collectible. Get ready to explore the attributes that make these coins valuable and learn how to differentiate them from the rest. The adventure has just begun, and the world of hidden treasures awaits your discovery.

Chapter 4: The Unexpected 1977 Quarter

As we embark on our journey to explore valuable coins hiding in plain sight, let's start by uncovering the story of a seemingly ordinary coin with a surprising secret. In this chapter, we'll delve into the details of the 1977 quarter – a coin with a common date but an uncommon feature that can turn it into a valuable find.

At first glance, the 1977 quarter might not seem much different from any other quarter. Its date is unremarkable, and its design is familiar. However, within this sea of 1977 quarters lies a hidden treasure – a coin with a unique attribute that sets it apart from its counterparts.

What makes the 1977 quarter special is its composition. While most quarters minted after 1964 are made of copper-nickel clad, this quarter was struck on a 40% silver planchet. This means it contains a portion of silver, distinguishing it from the typical circulation quarters. The significance lies in the silver content and the rarity of finding such a coin in everyday pocket change.

The key to identifying these silver quarterlies is the minting process. While 1977 quarters were predominantly struck in copper-nickel clad, some were accidentally minted on silver planchets. You need to look for the "S" mintmark on the coin to differentiate these silver quarters from their common counterparts. Quarters minted in San Francisco that bear the "S" mintmark are the ones to scrutinize.

In this chapter, we've introduced you to the concept of a common date coin holding extraordinary value. The 1977 silver quarter is just the tip of the iceberg – a reminder that careful observation and a willingness to learn can lead to remarkable discoveries. In the chapters, we'll explore more coins that defy expectations, turning everyday pocket change into unexpected wealth. Stay with us as we unravel the secrets hidden within the world of numismatics, one coin at a time.

CHAPTER 5: THE ICONIC 1969 DOUBLE DIE PENNY

Welcome to a chapter that delves into the world of numismatic anomalies, where coins take on a unique character that sets them apart from the ordinary. In this segment, we'll explore the captivating story behind the 1969 double-die penny – a coin that showcases the fascinating art of minting errors and their unexpected value.

When we think of coins, we often imagine pristine, perfectly struck images. However, the world of numismatics is filled with surprises, including coins with doubled images. The 1969 double-die penny is a prime example of this phenomenon – a coin that defies the conventions of minting precision.

In the minting process, errors can occur that lead to a coin having doubled images, creating a unique and fascinating effect. The doubling can be dramatic, with design elements appearing to be replicated or shifted. These errors are not the result of duplication but rather an unintended quirk that captures the attention of collectors and enthusiasts.

This chapter focuses on the 1969 penny, a seemingly common coin that carries an uncommon secret. The double die variety of this penny features distinct doubling on various elements of its design, making it a standout in any collection. The most notable doubling is visible in the phrases "In God We Trust," "Liberty," and the date "1969."

As with any collectible, the coin's condition is crucial in determining its value. The 1969 double-die penny in mint condition commands significantly higher prices than those in lesser condition. The interplay between rarity and grade creates a dynamic pricing structure that reflects the uniqueness of each coin.

In exploring the story of the 1969 double-die penny, we've opened the door to a world of minting anomalies and their captivating allure. The coins we handle daily possess stories far from ordinary, and each coin's journey from the mint to our pockets is an intricate tale waiting to be uncovered. In the subsequent chapters, we'll continue to unravel the stories of coins that hold secrets, turning our attention to coins that could transform your perspective on pocket change forever.

CHAPTER 6: THE VALUABLE 1992 CLOSE AM PENNY

Prepare to journey into subtle variations that can turn a common coin into a numismatic gem. In this chapter, we delve into the story of the 1992 close AM penny, an unassuming coin with a small but significant difference that elevates its value beyond its face.

Numismatics often revolves around nuances that escape the casual observer. The 1992 close AM penny is a prime example of how a minor difference can lead to an extraordinary value. This coin challenges us to look beyond the surface and discover the hidden tales within our pocket change.

The "AM" in "AMERICA" on the reverse side of the penny refers to the distance between the letters. In the case of the 1992 close AM penny case, the letters "A" and "M" are noticeably closer together than the standard variety. This minute difference may be easy to miss at first glance, but its impact on value is far from negligible.

As with many valuable coins, rarity plays a significant role in determining the worth of the 1992 close AM penny. While millions of 1992 pennies were minted, those with the close AM variety are a small subset. This scarcity, combined with the distinct feature, gives the coin a unique appeal that collectors eagerly seek.

As always, the condition of a coin profoundly affects its value. Like any collectible, the 1992 close AM penny commands higher prices when preserved in a mint state. Factors such as wear, blemishes, and overall appearance contribute to a coin's grade, influencing its market price.

As we unravel the story of the 1992 close AM penny, we are reminded that curiosity drives the world of numismatics. Small details that might escape our notice at first become the center of attention for collectors and enthusiasts. The chapter ahead will continue to shed light on coins with stories and attributes waiting to be discovered. Join us as we dive deeper into the treasures hidden within the world of pocket change.

CHAPTER 7: THE REMARKABLE 1995 DOUBLE DIE PENNY

Step into the world of doubled imagery and intricate errors as we delve into the story of the 1995 double-die penny. In this chapter, we'll explore how a subtle anomaly on a seemingly ordinary coin can transform it into a prized possession sought after by collectors and enthusiasts alike.

Coins with doubled images might seem like a quirk of the minting process, but they represent a fascinating realm within numismatics. The 1995 double die penny invites us to explore the beauty that can emerge from minting anomalies, turning ordinary coins into visual marvels.

Doubled die coins are the result of an error during the minting process. Elements of the design are imprinted twice, creating a distinctive effect that captures the imagination. The doubling can vary in intensity, from subtle to extreme, and can appear on various parts of the coin's design.

This chapter focuses on the 1995 penny, an intriguing double-die variety coin. The most prominent doubling occurs in the lettering, particularly in the word "LIBERTY." The doubling is not a mere smudge or imperfection; it's a tangible, intentional aspect of the coin's design that sets it apart.

As with any coin, the value of the 1995 double-die penny is influenced by factors such as grade and rarity. Coins in higher grades – those with minimal wear and well-preserved details – command greater prices among collectors. Combined with the distinct nature of the error, rarity contributes to the coin's allure.

The journey through the world of numismatics is a testament to the incredible diversity present even within a single denomination and year. The 1995 double-die penny reminds us that every coin has a unique story to tell and that these stories can range from the historical context of their mintage to the intriguing errors that set them apart.

As we conclude this chapter, remember that the coins we handle carry stories beyond their metal composition and face value. The allure of numismatics lies in discovering these stories and appreciating the intricate details that make each coin extraordinary. In the chapters ahead, we'll continue our exploration of coins that challenge our perception of pocket change and redefine their worth. Stay with us as we journey deeper into the world of hidden treasures and remarkable discoveries.

CHAPTER 8: THE UNEXPECTED RARITY OF THE 1968 SILVER DIME

Get ready to dive into a tale of unintended rarity as we explore the intriguing journey of the 1968 silver dime. In this chapter, we'll unravel how a coin from a year not known for silver content became a valuable treasure due to an unexpected twist in minting history.

While silver dimes were common in the United States before 1965, but the 1968 dime was not intended to be one of them. However, within numismatics, the unexpected is often where the greatest stories unfold. The 1968 silver dime challenges assumptions and showcases the fascinating complexities of coin minting.

In the minting world, even minor deviations can lead to monumental outcomes. The 1968 silver dime is a prime example of this principle. During a year when most dimes were transitioning to copper-nickel clad, a small number were minted on the traditional 90% silver planchet. This unique composition, unintentional as it was, created an immediate scarcity.

Identifying the 1968 silver dime is relatively straightforward – it weighs 2.5 grams, the standard weight for a silver dime. By comparison, the non-silver dimes of that era weighed 2.268 grams. This difference in weight serves as a clear indicator of the dime's unexpected silver content.

The rarity of the 1968 silver dime has transformed it from a coin of modest value to one sought after by collectors and enthusiasts. The interplay between rarity and historical anomaly has contributed to its appeal, making it a prized possession for those who recognize its significance.

As we explore the remarkable story of the 1968 silver dime, we're reminded that the world of numismatics is a realm of constant discovery. Every coin carries a tale; some tales are more unexpected than others. The next chapter will continue our journey, introducing us to coins that defy convention and remind us that even the most ordinary objects can hold extraordinary value. Stay tuned as we unveil the hidden treasures lurking within the world of pocket change.

CHAPTER 9: THE EXTRAORDINARY 2004 WISCONSIN STATE QUARTER

Prepare to embark on a journey through history and design as we uncover the captivating story of the 2004 Wisconsin State Quarter. In this chapter, we'll delve into how a coin designed to celebrate a state's heritage became a symbol of numismatic intrigue, capturing the imagination of collectors worldwide.

State quarters introduced a new era of coinage, where each state was commemorated with a unique design on the reverse side of the quarter. Among these, the 2004 Wisconsin State Quarter stands out for its striking imagery and a fascinating error that turned it into an extraordinary collectible.

The reverse design of the 2004 Wisconsin State Quarter features a depiction of a cow, a wheel of cheese, and an ear of corn – symbols of the state's agricultural heritage. However, within the intricate design lies an unexpected anomaly that took the numismatic world by storm.

A few of the 2004 Wisconsin State Quarters were minted with an additional leaf on the left side of the ear of corn. This error, known as the "extra leaf" variety, turned an otherwise accurate design into an enigma that collectors eagerly sought. The error was discovered on coins from both the Philadelphia and Denver Mints.

Identifying the extra leaf variety requires a keen eye and a willingness to scrutinize the design. The additional leaf can be seen between the two primary leaves of corn, creating a subtle but significant difference that sets these coins apart from their common counterparts.

The rarity of the extra leaf variety transformed the 2004 Wisconsin State Quarter from a simple commemorative coin into a numismatic sensation. Collectors and enthusiasts quickly recognized the allure of owning a piece of this unusual error, leading to increased demand and elevated prices.

As we journey through the 2004 Wisconsin State Quarter story, we're reminded that even in the world of modern coinage, surprises, and treasures can be found. Coins carry the stories of the times in which they were minted, and sometimes, these stories take unexpected twists that forever shape their value and significance. Join us as we continue our exploration of coins that challenge convention and redefine the notion of hidden treasures within our midst.

CHAPTER 10: THE UNIQUE 2009 DISTRICT OF COLUMBIA QUARTER

Welcome to a chapter that invites you to uncover a hidden gem nestled within the fascinating world of coinage – the 2009 District of Columbia quarter. In this segment, we'll explore how a coin designed to commemorate history took an unexpected turn and became a sought-after collectible due to a remarkable minting error.

The United States Mint embarked on a unique series of quarters in 2009, known as the "DC & US Territories" series, celebrating the District of Columbia and the US territories. Among these coins, the 2009 District of Columbia quarter stands out for a reason beyond its historical significance.

The 2009 District of Columbia quarter features a reverse design that depicts celebrated jazz musician Duke Ellington seated at a piano. However, some coins were minted with a remarkable error known as the "double die reverse." This error creates a doubling effect on specific design elements, making them stand out from their common counterparts.

To identify the double-die reverse variety, one must focus on the lettering and details of the coin's design. The doubling effect creates a slightly blurred or offset appearance in certain areas, such as Duke Ellington's last name and the piano keys. This distinctive error adds a layer of intrigue to the coin's already historical significance.

Minting errors have a unique way of capturing the imagination of collectors. The 2009 District of Columbia quarter with the double die reverse is a testament to the allure of coins that deviate from the norm. The charm lies not just in the historical story the coin tells but in the unexpected twist that makes it even more intriguing.

As with many error coins, the rarity and uniqueness of the 2009 District of Columbia quarter contribute to its value. Collectors are drawn to coins with anomalies or features that set them apart. The chapter ahead will continue to shed light on coins that challenge our assumptions and remind us that even within modern coinage, treasures can be found by those willing to look beyond the surface. Join us as we journey further into the world of hidden numismatic wonders.

CHAPTER 11: THE ENIGMATIC 1943 COPPER PENNY

Step into the realm of historical anomalies and unexpected rarities as we delve into the intriguing story of the 1943 copper penny. In this chapter, we'll explore how a coin that defied its era's norm became a prized possession among collectors, embodying the essence of numismatic fascination.

The year 1943 marked a significant shift in coin production due to World War II's demands for copper. In response, the U.S. Mint produced pennies using zinc-coated steel to conserve the precious metal. However, within this sea of wartime change emerged an anomaly that would capture the attention of numismatists for decades to come.

While most 1943 pennies were struck in zinc-coated steel, a small number were mistakenly minted on copper planchets intended for the previous year's coinage. These copper pennies, known as the "1943 copper cents," are a rare and captivating example of minting error.

Identifying the 1943 copper penny requires a discerning eye and a willingness to investigate its authenticity. The coin's date, weight, and magnetic properties are crucial indicators in differentiating the copper cent from its more common steel counterparts. The rarity of the 1943 copper cent elevates it to a prized find in the world of coin collecting.

The 1943 copper penny is a testament to the unexpected journeys that coins can take. What should have been a common wartime issue became a scarce and valuable anomaly due to a combination of errors and historical context. Collectors recognize the uniqueness of the 1943 copper cent and treasure it as a piece of numismatic history.

As we delve into the story of the 1943 copper penny, we're reminded that the world of numismatics is brimming with surprises. Coins hold stories that transcend their metal composition and face value, and the 1943 copper cent exemplifies how a simple coin can become a symbol of unexpected beauty and historical significance. Join us in the final chapters as we explore coins that challenge convention and invite us to see a pocket change in a new light.

CHAPTER 12: THE HIDDEN 1983 COPPER PENNY

Welcome to a chapter that uncovers the mysteries beneath the surface of coinage – the story of the 1983 copper penny. In this segment, we'll delve into how a seemingly ordinary coin can hide a valuable secret, challenging our perceptions and inviting us to question what we know about pocket change.

In the early 1980s, the U.S. Mint transitioned from striking pennies with traditional bronze to copper-plated zinc composition. However, within this transition lies a hidden treasure – the 1983 copper penny- waiting to be discovered.

While most 1983 pennies were struck on copper-plated zinc planchets, a small number were inadvertently struck on leftover bronze planchets from the previous year. These "1983 copper transitional error" pennies are a remarkable anomaly that challenges our assumptions about modern coinage.

Identifying the 1983 copper penny requires careful examination. The copper planchet gives these coins a distinct color and sheen, setting them apart from their zinc counterparts. These errors are often more apparent in their appearance and feel, making them an exciting find for collectors and enthusiasts.

The 1983 copper penny is a testament to how a simple mistake can transform an everyday object into something extraordinary. The rarity of this transitional error elevates its value beyond its face worth, reminding us that coins can hold hidden stories and surprises.

As we explore the intriguing tale of the 1983 copper penny, we're reminded that the world of numismatics is rich with hidden treasures waiting to be unearthed. Coins carry a history that extends beyond their minting, and anomalies like the 1983 copper penny challenge us to question our assumptions and discover the beauty within the mundane. Join us in the upcoming chapters as we continue to explore coins that redefine their worth and inspire us to see pocket change through a new lens.

CHAPTER 13: THE SOUGHT-AFTER 1955 DOUBLE DIE PENNY

Welcome to a chapter that uncovers a numismatic marvel that has captivated collectors for decades – the 1955 Double Die Penny. In this segment, we'll delve into the distinctive features that make this coin exceptional and explore the premium value that rare and well-preserved coins like these can command.

1955 brought forth a penny that would defy expectations and become a legendary coin in the numismatic world. The 1955 Double Die Penny is characterized by a doubling effect on its design elements, creating a visual effect that stands out from its standard counterparts. The doubling is particularly evident in the inscriptions "LIBERTY," "IN GOD WE TRUST," and the date "1955."

Identifying the 1955 Double Die Penny requires an appreciation for the subtle nuances that set it apart. The doubling effect, which is most pronounced on the obverse, gives the coin a distinct and captivating appearance. While most coins of the same era bear a single, clear design, the 1955 Double Die Penny challenges our perceptions and invites us to look beyond the surface.

Coins like the 1955 Double Die Penny are highly sought after due to their rarity and unique characteristics. Collectors recognize the premium value of coins that deviate from the norm, particularly when they are well-preserved. Condition plays a pivotal role in determining the value of a coin, and well-preserved examples of the 1955 Double Die Penny can command significant prices on the market.

The 1955 Double Die Penny serves as a testament to the intricate artistry of coin production and the unpredictable nature of minting errors. While most coins are produced with meticulous precision, errors like the double die remind us that even in the world of mass production, anomalies can emerge that transform ordinary coins into extraordinary collectibles.

As we delve into the captivating narrative of the 1955 Double Die Penny, we're reminded that numismatics is a celebration of diversity and unexpected beauty. Rare and well-preserved coins, especially those with unique errors, hold a special place in the hearts of collectors. Join us as we conclude our exploration with a reflection on the enduring allure of numismatic treasures and the endless possibilities they present to collectors and enthusiasts alike.

CHAPTER 14: THE EXCEPTIONAL 1959 BENT, DOUBLE-STRUCK PENNY

Welcome to a chapter that uncovers the remarkable story of a coin that defies convention – the 1959 Bent Double-Struck Penny. In this segment, we'll explore how a combination of errors turned an ordinary penny into an extraordinary numismatic rarity, showcasing the incredible value that distinct and uncommon errors can bring to a collection.

The 1959 penny is an iconic coin of its era, but not all share the same story. Imagine a penny that has undergone not one but two strikes by the coin press, resulting in a captivating doubling effect. On top of this, picture a penny struck with such force that it became bent during the striking process. The convergence of these errors transforms an everyday coin into an anomaly that demands attention.

Identifying the 1959 Bent Double-Struck Penny is an exercise in appreciation for the unexpected. The coin's distinctive features – the visible bending and the doubling of the design – create an immediately eye-catching and unique appearance. To truly grasp the rarity and value of this coin, one must consider the intricate combination of errors that brought it into existence.

Collectors often seek out errors due to their distinctiveness and the stories they tell. The 1959 Bent Double-Struck Penny is a testament to the allure of coins that deviate from the norm. This coin's value extends beyond its face worth, reflecting the rarity and complexity of the errors that shape its appearance.

Coins like the 1959 Bent Double-Struck Penny provide a unique glimpse into the inner workings of the minting process. They remind us that even within mass production machinery, there's room for unexpected beauty and anomalies that captivate the imagination.

As we explore the fascinating tale of the 1959 Bent Double-Struck Penny, we're reminded that numismatics celebrates the diversity and unpredictability of coinage. Uncommon errors showcase the ingenuity of minting, design intricacies, and imperfection's value. Join us in our concluding thoughts as we reflect on the enduring allure of numismatic treasures and the boundless possibilities they hold for collectors and enthusiasts alike.

CHAPTER 15: THE FASCINATING 1983 COPPER PLANCHET PENNY

Welcome to a chapter that delves into the world of numismatic anomalies and hidden treasures – the 1983 Copper Planchet Penny. In this segment, we'll explore the significance of a penny struck on a copper planchet during a transitional year, shedding light on the unique value such coins hold within coin collecting.

1983 marked a pivotal period in coin production as the U.S. Mint transitioned from striking pennies with traditional bronze to copper-plated zinc composition. Within this transition, a few coins escaped the norm and were struck on copper planchets – a rare occurrence that makes these coins a remarkable find for collectors.

Identifying the 1983 Copper Planchet Penny requires a keen eye for detail and a recognition of its distinct characteristics. These pennies exhibit a copper appearance that distinguishes them from their zinc-plated counterparts. Each coin became a tangible link to a specific moment in the Mint's history when changes were underway, making them an intriguing and sought-after addition to any collection.

Coins struck during transitional years, when the Mint adjusts its processes or materials, often hold a special place in the hearts of collectors. The 1983 Copper Planchet Penny is not just a testament to rarity but also a window into the complexities of coin production. Mint errors and anomalies provide a fascinating glimpse into the evolution of coinage.

The 1983 Copper Planchet Penny serves as a reminder that coins are not mere currency; they are artifacts that embody history, art, and human craftsmanship. The rarity of these coins extends their value beyond face worth, reflecting their unique place in numismatic history and the curiosity they evoke among collectors.

As we delve into the captivating narrative of the 1983 Copper Planchet Penny, we're reminded that the world of coin collecting is a journey of discovery. Uncommon errors, transitional anomalies, and hidden treasures challenge us to look beyond the ordinary and embrace the unexpected. Join us as we conclude our exploration with a reflection on the enduring allure of numismatic treasures and the limitless possibilities they offer to collectors and enthusiasts alike.

CHAPTER 16: THE RARE 1998 PROOF PENNY ERROR

Welcome to a chapter that uncovers a numismatic anomaly that showcases the unexpected twists that coins can take – the Rare 1998 Proof Penny Error. In this segment, we'll dive into the significance of a proof penny from 1998 that carries errors, offering insights into the world of proof coinage and highlighting the distinct qualities that set proof coins apart from their business strike counterparts.

Proof coins are struck with meticulous care and attention to detail, making them prized pieces in numismatics. The year 1998 brought forth a proof penny that stood out not just for its exceptional finish but for the errors that were unintentionally stamped onto its surface, adding an unexpected layer of intrigue.

The Rare 1998 Proof Penny Error is a coin that demonstrates the complexities of coin production. Minting errors, even within the realm of proof coinage, are a reminder that perfection is a rare feat. The errors on this coin – whether they involve doubling, misalignments, or other anomalies – provide a unique perspective on the intricacies of the minting process.

Understanding the differences between proof and business strike coins is crucial to appreciating the significance of the 1998 Proof Penny Error. Proof coins are struck with specially polished dies on polished planchets, resulting in sharp details, mirror-like fields, and frosted designs. On the other hand, business strike coins are produced for circulation and exhibit a more standard appearance.

The Rare 1998 Proof Penny Error is a testament that numismatic value is not solely based on perfection. Coins with errors, especially those within proof coinage, hold a unique charm for collectors. Their rarity, combined with the exquisite finish of proof coins, elevates their appeal and positions them as sought-after additions to any collection.

Coins like the 1998 Proof Penny Error offer a window into the inner workings of the minting process. They remind us that even the most carefully orchestrated production can give rise to anomalies that intrigue collectors and spark conversations about the artistry and technology behind coin creation.

As we conclude our exploration of the Rare 1998 Proof Penny Error, we're reminded that the world of numismatics is a journey filled with unexpected twists and hidden treasures. Proof coins, errors, and the convergence of the two invited us to celebrate the nuances that make each coin a unique piece of history. Join us as we reflect on the allure of numismatic discoveries and the boundless fascination they offer collectors and enthusiasts worldwide.

CHAPTER 17: THE UNIQUE DOLLAR-PRESIDENTIAL QUARTER MULE

Welcome to a chapter that delves into the world of numismatic anomalies that challenge convention – the Unique Dollar-Presidential Quarter Mule. In this segment, we'll unravel the fascinating concept of a mule coin, where the design of a dollar coin meets that of a quarter, and we'll explore the rarity and value of these remarkable and unusual numismatic combinations.

Imagine a coin that bridges the gap between denominations, merging the design of a dollar coin with that of a presidential quarter. The Unique Dollar-Presidential Quarter Mule takes the art of coin design to a whole new level by fusing the familiar features of both coins into a single, captivating piece.

Mule coins are intriguing anomalies that result from a mix-up in the minting process, combining elements from different coin types or denominations. These errors, while unintended, create coins that stand out from the crowd and offer collectors a glimpse into the unpredictable nature of minting.

The rarity of mule coins, especially those that combine unusual pairings like a dollar coin with a quarter design, makes them highly sought after by collectors. The unexpected convergence of designs and denominations adds intrigue and uniqueness, setting these coins apart from their more-traditional counterparts.

The Unique Dollar-Presidential Quarter Mule showcases how coins can transcend their monetary value and become artifacts that tell a story of innovation, human error, and artistic exploration. The value of these mule coins extends beyond their face worth, reflecting their status as numismatic treasures that encapsulate a specific moment in the history of coin production.

As we explore the captivating narrative of the Unique Dollar-Presidential Quarter Mule, we're reminded that numismatics celebrates the unexpected and the creative. Mule coins offer us a glimpse into the complexity of coin production and the limitless possibilities that can emerge when elements align unexpectedly.

As we conclude our journey through the world of numismatic anomalies, we invite you to embrace the uniqueness and diversity that coins can offer. The Unique Dollar-Presidential Quarter Mule reminds us that even within the realm of coinage, there's room for exploration, error, and extraordinary beauty. Join us in our final reflections as we celebrate the allure of numismatic treasures and the endless fascination they hold for collectors and enthusiasts around the world.

CONCLUSION: EMBRACING THE WORLD OF VALUABLE COINS IN YOUR POCKET CHANGE

In this mini ebook, we embarked on a captivating journey through the world of numismatic treasures that could be hiding in your very own pocket change. We explored a diverse array of coins, each with its own unique story and value. Let's take a moment to recap the key points we've covered and reflect on the exciting possibilities within your everyday coins.

Throughout these chapters, we've discovered the hidden potential within seemingly ordinary coins. From quarters struck on unexpected planchets to pennies with remarkable errors, each coin has the power to carry a story of rarity, uniqueness, and historical significance.

We've explored coins that defy convention, like the 1955 Double Die Penny and the 1983 Copper Planchet Penny, showcasing the extraordinary beauty that can emerge from minting errors. We've delved into the world of proof coins and transitional years, shedding light on the factors that elevate certain coins to the status of numismatic gems.

We've also marveled at the intriguing anomalies like mule coins and merged designs, highlighting the creative potential within coin production. And through it all, we've emphasized the value of staying vigilant, exploring, and seeking out the hidden treasures that may be waiting right in your pocket change.

As we conclude our exploration, we encourage you to embrace the spirit of discovery and curiosity that numismatics offers. Every coin you encounter, whether in your pocket, your wallet, or a roll from the bank, has the potential to hold more than just monetary value. It could be a rare error, a transitional piece, or a unique anomaly that sets it apart.

Continue to stay vigilant and keep an eye out for the valuable coins that could be circulating right under your nose. Equip yourself with knowledge about different coin errors, designs, and historical contexts. Consider investing in tools like magnifying glasses or microscopes to enhance your ability to spot these hidden treasures.

Remember that the journey of collecting coins is about amassing monetary wealth and connecting with history, artistry, and the ever-evolving world of numismatics. The coins in your pocket change are like windows into different eras, reflecting the complexities and stories of their time.

Thank you for joining us to explore valuable coins in your pocket change. As you continue your numismatic adventure, may you uncover rare gems, share your discoveries with fellow enthusiasts, and find joy in the intriguing world of numismatic treasures. Happy collecting!

BOOK 7 - COINS VS BARS

CHAPTER 1

INTRODUCTION TO PRECIOUS METAL INVESTMENTS: COINS VS. BARS

Investing in precious metals is a time-tested strategy for safeguarding wealth and diversifying portfolios. Two primary choices emerge when delving into the world of precious metal investing: coins and bars. In this chapter, we will embark on a journey to uncover the fundamental differences between these two investment forms. By understanding the unique attributes of coins and bars, you'll be better equipped to make informed decisions that align with your financial goals.

1.1: DECIPHERING THE LURE OF PRECIOUS METALS

Embarking on a journey into investing in precious metals is like setting off on a captivating adventure filled with deep meaning. These precious treasures, like coins and bars made from gold, silver, platinum, and palladium, have magic beyond their monetary value. They're like windows to the past, holding stories from different times and cultures. In this section, we'll uncover what makes these metals so special, showing how getting involved with them is like discovering a treasure chest of stories that go through history and leave a lasting mark for the future.

Imagine holding an old gold coin that people used ages ago or a piece of silver that changed hands during a critical historical moment. These coins have marks from kings, leaders, and civilizations, making them a connection to days long gone. The art and skill of making these coins connect you to how things looked and what was important back then. When you hold these old coins, you're not just holding metal but also stories of people and cultures that shaped our world.

Underneath the shiny surface of coins, there's another exciting part: bars. These solid blocks of precious metal mean more than just their weight and what they're made of. These bars show how we've used precious metals to create things that move our world forward, like technology. Imagine holding a bar of platinum or palladium – it's like holding a piece of the technology that changed the world. These bars are like the building blocks of machines, electronics, and new technologies that are important today.

The appeal of precious metals isn't just about how coins look or what bars do – it's about their value and safety. Throughout history, gold and silver have been considered safe places to put money, especially when things are uncertain in the economy or the world. Precious metals stay strong when regular money struggles and things like stocks and paper money are shaky. This tells us that people believe in their values no matter what's happening around them. This strength shows that these assets are special because they don't just follow trends or economic ups and downs.

The fascination with precious metals isn't limited to one group of people or one place – it's something people worldwide understand and appreciate.

For example, gold has been used by powerful rulers in religious ceremonies and to show status. This makes your investment something that connects to people no matter where they're from. It's like a language that everyone understands because these shiny metals have a universal appeal.

When you start looking into investing in precious metals, you're doing more than just making choices about money. It's like going on a journey that helps you connect with history, different cultures, and the value that's important for generations. By understanding why these tangible things are so special, you're getting ready to make smart investment decisions and learning about how value, history, and human experiences are all linked. As you learn and make choices in this world, remember that the magic of precious metals reflects the magic of life itself – where value and importance shine through in every part of our existence.

1.2: Unveiling the Investment Potential

Before examining coins and bars, let's dig into why people are drawn to investing in precious metals. These solid assets have a special appeal that goes beyond just looking nice. They're highly valued for their investment potential and the many advantages they offer to those who want to secure their finances.

One of the biggest benefits of precious metals is that they act as a strong shield against the ups and downs of the economy. These days, financial markets can be unpredictable, with unexpected changes happening. Precious metals provide a stable anchor during these uncertain times. Because they have a real, physical value, even if the market goes down, the value of your investment stays strong.

Another concern that comes up a lot is the loss of buying power when money loses value. Precious metals, though, don't have this problem. When central banks print more money and prices, increase, the value of things like gold, silver, platinum, and palladium stays the same. This means your investment keeps its value, even if the money's value is changing.

The financial world can get shaken up when there's political trouble or conflicts between countries. Precious metals are like a safe place to spend money during these times. They're valuable no matter where you are or what's going on politically. This stability can help protect your wealth when things get uncertain globally.

What makes investing in precious metals even more attractive is that they've been valuable for a really long time. Throughout history, empires and economies have come and gone, but the value of metals like gold and silver has always stayed. This shows how well they can preserve wealth across many generations. Investing in precious metals means following a practice that's stood the test of time.

Adding precious metals to your investments can make your strategy stronger. Regular assets like stocks and bonds can change much based on the market and economy. But precious metals don't follow those same patterns. This means that if things get tough in the market, your investments in metals can still hold steady. This mix helps protect your wealth against the unpredictable changes in today's economies.

In short, the benefits of precious metals go beyond their physical form. They're a way to guard against economic ups and downs, money-losing value, and uncertain times globally. They're a solid foundation for a well-balanced investment plan. As we look into coins and bars, remember that you're not just getting pieces of metal – you're adopting a smart way to protect your money and secure a stable financial future in a world that's always changing.

1.3: Defining the Path Ahead: Coins and Bars

When it comes to investing in precious metals, there are two main options: coins and bars. Each choice has its qualities and things to think about. Deciding between them means exploring what makes them different and what benefits they offer. This part is like a map that helps you understand the special features of coins and bars as investments. It guides you to make smart choices that match what you want to achieve with your investments.

Governments often make coins and have a story to tell beyond just their value. They hold history and art in them. When you own coins, you're kind of like a keeper of history. These coins can also become valuable because people collect them like art, and their value can go up over time.

On the other hand, bars, which private companies make, have a different purpose. They're solid pieces of metal that focus on being pure and useful. Bars are simpler than coins; their main value comes from the metal itself. They often cost less, so they're a good choice if you want to collect much metal without paying a premium.

When you're trying to choose between coins and bars, what you know is really important. Learning about what makes each option good helps you make the right choice for what you want. Do you like the stories that come with coins, or do you prefer the simple value of bars? Are you interested in the chance that coins become more valuable over time, or do you like bars because they're practical and easy to store?

In the end, your decision between coins and bars is a mix of what you find attractive and what works best for your goals. Coins connect you to history and art, while bars are about being pure and practical. The one you pick shows what you value most and what kind of investment strategy you like.

Looking at coins and bars opens up different possibilities, giving you a unique way to invest in precious metals. The stories of history, the beauty of art, and the simplicity of purity shape what coins and bars mean. This exploration makes your investment journey exciting and diverse. As you move forward, remember that your choice reflects your vision, goals, and what you like. By making informed decisions, you're paving a path toward a future that shines with the timeless value of precious metals.

1.4: THE JOURNEY AHEAD

As we explore coins and bars, keep in mind the shared attributes that form the foundation of both investments. The knowledge gained from understanding each product's manufacturer, weight, purity, and metal type serves as a cornerstone upon which we will build our insights. Armed with this understanding, we will journey deeper into precious metal investing, unveiling the nuances that set coins and bars apart and guiding you toward making confident investment decisions that align with your aspirations.

CHAPTER 2: COMMON FEATURES OF COINS AND BARS

When investing in precious metals, coins and bars have essential things in common that make them valuable and interesting. As we start this section, we'll explore these shared features that connect these two different ways of investing. We'll uncover the important things that all investors should know about.

2.1: IDENTIFYING THE SOURCE: MANUFACTURER INFORMATION

In the world of investing in precious metals, there's something that ties every coin and bar together, no matter how they look: the information about who made them. This might seem like just a detail, but it's important. It's like a special code that helps you know if the metal is real, where it came from, and how good it is. As we look into this topic, we'll dig into how this mark is more than just a name; it's like proof of the history, skill, and trust that comes with the metal.

Imagine you have a coin with a stamp from a country or a bar with a mark from a private company. That mark is like a guarantee that the metal is genuine. It's a way to show that the people who know about this stuff have given it a thumbs up. When a country makes coins, they want to ensure each coin is just right, inside and out. Private companies making bars want to make them really pure and top-notch, and their mark is like a sign of that quality.

The coins from countries aren't just about money; they also have cool designs that show off things like historical figures, symbols, and stuff from that country's culture. The mark about who made the coin shows that the country cares about its history and values. Holding one of these coins is like holding a piece of that country's story.

Private companies that make bars play a different role. They're not connected to the government but are still super important. The mark they put on their bars says, "We made this, and we're serious about making it top-quality." These companies are known for making bars that you can trust.

That information about who made the precious metal isn't just a name on a tag. It guarantees that your investment is the real deal and good quality. This is a big deal today because there are fake things out there that look real. When you know what this mark means, you protect your investment and ensure you're getting what you paid for. You also respect the skill and honesty of the people who made it.

As you dive deeper into investing in precious metals, remember that each piece you hold isn't just a thing; it's like a sign that you trust the metal and the people behind it. The information about who made the coin or bar isn't just a label; it's like a seal of trust, a symbol of quality, and a promise that it's genuine. By understanding the importance of this mark, you're ready to make smart decisions that match your investment goals. You can be confident that each piece you get comes with a reliable history.

2.2: WEIGHING THE SIGNIFICANCE: WEIGHT OF THE PRODUCT

In the complex world of investing in precious metals, the weight of each piece means more than just a number – it holds deep meaning that goes through history, trade, and understanding value. Both coins and bars proudly show their weight, usually in troy ounces or grams. These are like a common language for precious metals, helping investors know how much they have. Knowing the weight doesn't just tell you how heavy it is; it also tells you how valuable it is, connecting you to the heart of precious metal investing.

In the world of precious metals, troy ounces and grams are like the way everyone talks about value. It doesn't matter where you are or where you're from – these measurements are like a shared understanding of how valuable something is. Troy ounces are different from regular ounces and have a long history, making sure that the value of precious metals is clear and the same across the world.

The weight of a precious metal product decides how valuable it is. Bigger and heavier pieces are worth more because they have more of the precious metal in them. This direct link between weight and value is important when deciding where to invest your money. It shows why understanding the weight of what you have is key.

Looking at the weight of your precious metal investment connects you to its actual value. Whether holding a coin or a bar, the weight tells you how much of the metal is in there. This weight is like the heart of the metal's value, staying the same even when things are changing in the market.

The weight of the product doesn't change over time or place. It's a consistent way to know how much something is worth. This helps everyone understand how much your investment is worth, no matter when they're looking at it. This shows how precious metals are valuable for a long time.

As you explore the world of investing in precious metals, the weight of each piece is like a real representation of its value. Whether you have a coin or a bar, its weight shows how much the precious metal is worth. This doesn't change even when the market is moving around. Understanding why weight matters gives you an important tool to know and appreciate your investments. It's like holding the value itself in your hand.

2.3: Pure Essence: Purity of the Precious Metal

In the world of investing in precious metals, something really important lies at the heart of it all—the pureness of the metal itself. Whether it's the shine of silver, the beautiful glow of gold, the understated elegance of platinum, or the mysterious charm of palladium, each product is proof of what it's made of. These products proudly show their purity levels, which say a lot about how real they are, how valuable, and how deeply they matter. Understanding purity takes us into a world where realness and attractiveness are tightly connected, forming the base of investing in precious metals.

In the world of precious metals, purity is like the truth detector. It's often shown as a number with a decimal point, like .999 or .9999. This number tells you how much of the valuable metal is actually in there. This sign of purity is like a promise that what you're holding is truly made of the precious metal it claims to be. This honesty eliminates doubts and gives you confidence that your investment is real and worth something that lasts.

When precious metal products have higher purity levels, they become even more captivating. A higher fineness means a bigger amount of the special metal in the mix. You can see this in the shine of gold, the gleam of silver, and the brightness of platinum and palladium. This higher concentration not only makes the product more valuable but also makes it rarer, which makes collectors, investors, and fans really interested in it.

In investing in precious metals, purity and value go hand in hand. The level of purity a product has directly affects how much it's worth. It's like a clear way to judge its value. The difference between something that's .999 pure and something .9999 pure isn't just about numbers; it shows how much of the metal is there and how much people want it. People in the market notice and value higher purity levels, showing the strong connection between purity and how much something is thought to be worth.

In today's world, where we can find information easily, knowing the purity of precious metal products adds trust to them. Whether you're getting a coin or a bar, understanding how pure it is gives you power. This knowledge helps you make smart choices about your investments. This trust, kept up by reliable mints and refineries, strengthens the bond between investors and precious metals.

As you dive into the world of investing in precious metals, the idea of purity shows you the bright center of every piece. It's not just about how much metal is there; it's proof of honesty, worth, and attractiveness that lasts through time. By understanding what purity means, you're not just realizing how valuable your investments are but also joining a common language of truth, trust, and lasting value that's always important.

2.4: Discerning the Essence: Type of Metal

As we dive deeper into investing in precious metals, we step into a realm where these valuable treasures come in different flavors. Beyond the shared things like who made them, how heavy they are, and how pure they are, coins and bars also tell us what they're made of. The kind of metal they're made from—like the shiny charm of silver, the timeless luxury of gold, the sturdy grace of platinum, or the mysterious elegance of palladium—adds a big dose of character to the product, showing us what it can do and what it's worth. Figuring out each metal is like discovering a whole bunch of traits that shape the story of your investment journey.

Each type of metal brings its own special thing to the world of precious metals. Silver, with its cool glow and how well it conducts electricity, has a sort of industrial appeal that goes from tech to photography. Gold, the picture of timeless richness, has been grabbing people's attention for ages, standing for riches, power, and art. Platinum's quiet style is super tough and doesn't corrode easily, making it important in many industries. Palladium, a newer member of the precious metal family, has its own charm and is finding more and more uses, from cleaning up car exhaust to being used in jewelry.

But the type of metal isn't just a way to classify them—it's also a storyteller. It has a say in how something looks, what kind of personality it has, and how strong it is. Gold's warm shine, silver's cool gleam, platinum's calm beauty, and palladium's shiny glow—all these colors paint a picture of your investment in exciting ways. But it's not just about looks; each metal has special qualities that make it tough enough to last through time, adding value.

Understanding the type of metal takes you through history and into the modern world. The history behind gold, the way platinum became a symbol of class, and how silver and palladium are used today—all these stories come together to define each metal. Knowing these stories helps you understand why each metal matters and how they fit into your investment plan, adding more layers to your collection and view.

As you journey into precious metal investments, figuring out which metal you're into is like picking a tune. Different metals attract different kinds of investors, each looking to put their spin on their investment plan. Are you into the luxury of gold, silver's versatility, platinum's elegance, or palladium's mystery? Your answer to this question shapes your investment journey, matching your choices with what you care about and where you want to go.

The type of metal isn't just a word; it's a story about history, looks, strength, and new ideas. By getting to know what makes each metal special, you're adding more layers to your investment journey. Whether you're interested in the story of the past, the sparkle of looks, or the promise of new things, the type of metal guides you toward different options, each one a chance to shape your investment collection and your own legacy.

2.5: A Unified Foundation

As we navigate the shared characteristics of coins and bars, we appreciate the foundational elements that tie these investments together. Manufacturer information, weight, purity, and type of metal stand as unifying pillars that transcend the boundaries of form and design. Whether you invest in the rich history of coins or the refined simplicity of bars, these common features serve as your guideposts, offering a clear path to understanding and maximizing the value of your precious metal investments. With this knowledge in hand, we'll explore the nuances that set coins and bars apart, empowering you to navigate the intricacies of the precious metals market with confidence and insight.

CHAPTER 3: CONSIDERATIONS WHEN BUYING PRECIOUS METALS

As you step into the realm of precious metal investing, many factors come into play, shaping your decisions and your path. This chapter delves into the essential considerations that should guide your purchasing journey. Whether you're drawn to the artistry of coins or the efficiency of bars, understanding the nuances of each option and the implications of your choices will empower you to make well-informed investment decisions.

3.1: NAVIGATING THE FORK: COINS OR BARS?

As you embark on your journey into the world of precious metal investments, a critical crossroads beckons—a choice that sets the tone for your investment narrative: coins or bars. Each path unfurls before you with its own allure, beckoning you to explore the nuances of history, aesthetics, and intrinsic value. The choice between coins and bars isn't merely a matter of aesthetics; it reflects your investment philosophy, aspirations, and the stories you wish to weave within your portfolio.

Coins, with their historical legacy and artistic charm, invite you to step into the corridors of time. Often minted by sovereign nations, these pieces bear the imprints of emperors, monarchs, and cultural symbols that have shaped civilizations. Holding a coin isn't just an investment; it's a tangible link to the past, a whisper of the stories that have echoed through generations. The artistic mastery that adorns coins transforms them into miniature canvases that capture the essence of their era. Coins reflect the metal's value and the rich tapestry of history.

In stark contrast, bars stand as embodiments of purity and core value. These sleek, streamlined pieces prioritize the essence of the precious metal itself, presenting it in its purest form. Bars often bear the hallmarks of their manufacturer and purity level, distilling their identity to the essential elements. The decision to invest in bars resonates with those who seek the raw, unadulterated value of precious metals without the ornamentation of historical narratives.

The choice between coins and bars unveils your investment philosophy. Are you drawn to the stories woven into history, the artistic expressions of civilizations past? Coins align with a philosophy that values the metal's worth and the stories that amplify its significance. Alternatively, do you resonate with the purity of value, prioritizing the core essence of precious metals? Bars reflect an investment philosophy that prioritizes the intrinsic value of the metal itself.

Universal rules don't govern the choice between coins and bars; your individual preferences and aspirations govern it. Perhaps you find solace in holding a coin that once passed through the hands of historical figures. Or maybe you're captivated by the pristine beauty of a bar that gleams with the assurance of purity. Your aspirations, goals, and desired connections to your investment shape this decision, aligning it with the essence of your journey.

Standing at the crossroads between coins and bars, you're poised to embrace a path that aligns with your investment vision. The choice isn't binary; it's a canvas where you paint your aspirations, values, and narratives. Whether you're drawn to the symphony of history or the purity of essence, your choice etches a unique mark on your investment journey. By understanding the distinct attributes of coins and bars, you're not just selecting a form; you're crafting a narrative that resonates with your journey, your goals, and the legacy you wish to leave behind.

3.2: The Producer's Imprint: Sovereign Mint vs. Private Refinery

In the landscape of precious metal production, two distinctive protagonists step onto the stage—the sovereign mint and the private refinery. Each entity wields its unique signature, crafting coins and bars that bear the weight of metal and the essence of history, culture, and purity. The choice between sovereign mints and private refineries extends beyond the physical attributes; it's a choice between narratives, values, and the legacy you wish to embrace within your investment journey.

As the name implies, sovereign mints carry the emblem of governmental authority. These entities are backed by nations, lending an air of authenticity and heritage to the products they produce. The coins minted by sovereign mints transcend their monetary value; they embody historical narratives, cultural symbols, and the collective identity of a nation. These coins aren't just precious metals; they're vessels of heritage that connect investors to the stories and milestones of civilizations. Holding a coin minted by a sovereign mint is akin to holding a piece of history, a tangible link to the legacy of a nation.

Conversely, private refineries channel their expertise into the production of bars, which stand as monuments of purity and efficiency. These bars, marked by their streamlined design and purity hallmark, spotlight the core essence of the precious metal. The emphasis is on the intrinsic value—the raw material—without the adornments of historical narratives. Private refineries cater to those seeking the elemental purity of precious metals, underscoring the universal worth transcending borders and civilizations.

The choice between sovereign mints and private refineries transcends the product's physical form; it rests upon the reputation and track record of the producer. Sovereign mints boast historical significance and governmental endorsement, ensuring the authenticity of their coins. Private refineries, on the other hand, differentiate themselves through a focus on purity and precision. Understanding the producer's reputation is paramount to a successful investment journey regardless of the path you choose.

Investors seeking credibility need not look far; the LBMA Good Delivery List and the Comex Good Delivery List are beacons of a producer's commitment to quality. These lists unveil the producers whose products adhere to rigorous purity, authenticity, and craftsmanship standards. A producer's inclusion in these prestigious lists signifies more than just compliance; it signifies a dedication to upholding the values that investors hold dear.

As you stand at the crossroads between sovereign mints and private refineries, you're engaging with a choice that transcends the tangible. It's a choice that echoes through time, connecting you with heritage, legacy, and the elemental essence of precious metals. Whether you're drawn to the narratives of sovereign coins or the purity of private bars, the decision is a reflection of your values, aspirations, and the stories you wish to carry within your investment journey. By understanding the significance of the producer's imprint, you're empowered to make choices that align with your vision, ensuring that your investment legacy is a testament to value and an ode to authenticity, heritage, and the spirit of the precious metal itself.

3.3: Finding the Perfect Fit: Size, Goals, and Premiums

As you navigate the intricate world of precious metal investments, the size of your investment emerges as a pivotal player on the stage of your portfolio. This dimension isn't just about ounces and grams; it's about striking a harmonious balance between size, goals, and premiums—a symphony where each note contributes to the overall composition of your investment journey. This exploration invites you to dance on the tightrope of choice, seeking the perfect fit that aligns with your aspirations and financial objectives.

In the realm of precious metals, size isn't just a numeric value; it's a matter of scale that influences your investment's physical and symbolic weight. Smaller sizes, such as fractional coins or bars, offer a touch of enchantment through their divisibility and flexibility. These diminutive marvels aren't just pieces of metal; they're tokens of potential transactions, exchanges, and even bartering—an asset that adapts to the changing rhythms of economic interactions.

On the other end of the spectrum, larger sizes—kilo bars and their ilk— command attention with their grandeur. Beyond their imposing presence, they often come with the allure of lower premiums per ounce. This financial alchemy transforms these bars into attractive options for those considering bulk investments. The promise of potentially paying less per unit of precious metal lures investors seeking economies of scale.

In this dance, your investment goals hold the compass that guides your steps. Are you seeking liquidity, the ability to swiftly convert your assets into cash if needed? Perhaps wealth preservation is your primary objective, a steadfast commitment to safeguarding value against economic fluctuations. Or maybe you're drawn by the siren call of potential appreciation—the allure of watching your investment grow in worth over time. Whatever your goals, they will influence the size you choose to invest in.

As you waltz through the realm of investment sizes, be prepared to face the weight of trade-offs. Smaller sizes may offer divisibility and versatility but often come with higher premiums per ounce. With their cost-efficient allure, larger sizes may limit liquidity due to their substantial worth. Each size carries its own set of benefits and considerations, requiring you to discern which trade-offs align best with your overarching vision.

In the symphony of investment, the size of your precious metal holdings forms a unique note that harmonizes with your goals, values, and financial aspirations. As you weave through the choices of fractional coins, kilo bars, and everything in between, remember that each size is a brushstroke on the canvas of your portfolio. By understanding the dance between size, goals, and premiums, you're orchestrating a composition that resonates with your investment philosophy, the legacy you wish to leave, and the financial journey you're crafting.

Understanding your options is key to making well-informed decisions in the intricate landscape of precious metal investments. Your unique goals, preferences, and circumstances will shape the path you tread, whether it leads to coins or bars, sovereign mints or private refineries, and fractional or larger sizes. Navigating the considerations outlined in this chapter lays the foundation for a well-rounded and strategic approach to your precious metal investments. Armed with this knowledge, you're ready to take the next step on your journey, equipped with the tools to create a portfolio that aligns with your financial aspirations.

Chapter 4: Brand Reputation and Resale Value

In the intricate world of precious metal investments, one factor stands out as a guiding beacon: brand reputation. The producer's reputation behind your chosen coins or bars carries profound implications for both your confidence in the investment and its potential resale value. This chapter delves into the significance of brand reputation and how it intertwines with the resale value of precious metal products.

4.1: A TRUSTED LEGACY: THE POWER OF BRAND REPUTATION

In the tapestry of industries, the concept of a brand goes beyond a mere label; it embodies a legacy of trust, quality, and assurance. Just as in the realms of technology, fashion, or automobiles, the precious metals arena is graced by the presence of reputable brands that stand as beacons of reliability and authenticity. These esteemed producers, whether sovereign mints or private refineries, wield a power that transcends the tangible; they are custodians of a trusted legacy, guardians of integrity in a market where trust holds unparalleled value.

In a world teeming with choices, reputable producers emerge as pillars of integrity—guardians of a code that upholds the highest standards of craftsmanship and quality. These entities, whether emblazoned with the emblem of a sovereign nation or the insignia of a private refinery, have earned their place as custodians of the precious metals arena. Their commitment to excellence echoes through their products, casting a halo of reliability that envelops each piece of metal they produce.

Investing in products from reputable producers isn't merely an exercise in due diligence; it's a testament to your pursuit of excellence. These brands do not merely meet expectations; they often exceed them, transforming each investment into a story of value, authenticity, and trust. When you acquire a coin minted by a sovereign mint or a bar refined by a private mint, you're not just acquiring metal; you're embracing a legacy—an assurance that your investment journey is anchored in the bedrock of quality.

The legacy of these brands is a symphony woven from the threads of trust. Just as a foundation supports a grand edifice, trust is the cornerstone upon which these brands have built their reputations. This trust is earned through meticulous adherence to stringent standards, uncompromising attention to detail, and an unswerving commitment to providing investors with products that stand as paragons of authenticity.

These reputable producers are natural allies for assurance for investors navigating the realm of precious metals. In a market where provenance and legitimacy are paramount, the products bearing the imprints of these brands radiate confidence that quells doubts and instills certainty. The coins and bars they produce are more than commodities; they are symbols of a legacy that spans generations, a legacy grounded in the unwavering trust of investors.

In the grand composition of the precious metals market, reputable brands play a melodious role—a symphony of trust that resonates through time. Their legacy isn't merely etched in metal; it's etched in the hearts and minds of investors who seek not just wealth, but also a legacy of authenticity and integrity. As you embrace coins minted by sovereign mints or bars refined by private refineries, you're not just acquiring precious metals; you're participating in a narrative—a narrative of trust, quality, and a commitment to the timeless pursuit of excellence.

4.2: LIQUIDITY AND RESALE VALUE: THE NEXUS OF TRUST

In the intricate dance of precious metal investments, liquidity, and resale value emerge as twin constellations that guide your journey. This cosmic relationship is rooted in the principle of trust, where the reputation of brands acts as the gravitational force that holds these celestial bodies in perfect alignment. As you delve deeper into this nexus, you'll uncover the ways in which brand reputation intertwines with liquidity and resale value to shape the destiny of your investment.

Imagine liquidity as the lifeblood coursing through the veins of your investments. It's the ability to transform your precious metal holdings into cash easily and swiftly. When the moment arrives to divest your investment, the liquidity of the products you hold determines how seamlessly you can transition from ownership to currency. And within this framework, the trust commanded by reputable brands becomes a beacon that illuminates your path.

Similar to the crescendo of a symphony, resale value marks the culmination of your investment journey. It's the price you receive when you part ways with your precious metal holdings. Here, the symphony comprises brand reputation, demand, and trust. Products that bear the imprints of established mints or refineries stand in the spotlight, their virtuoso performance instilling trust in potential buyers. This trust translates to demand, and demand, in turn, results in higher resale value.

The relationship between brand reputation and resale value is not a mere coincidence; it's a symbiotic dance where one complements and reinforces the other. Precious metal products from respected mints or refineries are infused with a higher degree of trust. This trust isn't just skin deep; it permeates the very essence of the metal. And as you venture to liquidate your investment, this trust resonates with potential buyers, casting a reassuring aura that eases their decisions.

In the bustling marketplace, where choices abound and decisions are fraught with considerations, the trust commanded by reputable brands is a competitive advantage. When you offer products with a legacy of trust, you give potential buyers a sense of security beyond the metal itself. This assurance translates to swifter decision-making and a willingness to pay a premium for the comfort of authenticity.

As you journey through the cosmos of precious metal investments, remember that liquidity and resale value are more than abstract concepts; they're tangible outcomes woven from the fabric of trust. The resonance of reputable brands with potential buyers forms an equation where trust equals liquidity equals higher resale value. By understanding this delicate interplay, you wield the power to make investment decisions that resonate with harmony, ensuring that your investment symphony culminates with the sweetest of notes—a competitive price for your holdings, a legacy of trust, and a journey illuminated by authenticity.

4.3: THE LBMA AND COMEX GOOD DELIVERY LISTS

Two guiding stars emerge in the constellation of precious metal investments: the LBMA (London Bullion Market Association) Good Delivery List and the Comex (Commodity Exchange) Good Delivery List. These celestial references stand as beacons of reliability and authenticity, casting a reassuring light on the path of investors seeking quality and trust. As you peer into the night sky of precious metal investment, these lists shine bright, illuminating a world where credibility and market acceptance converge.

Credibility is the cornerstone upon which the LBMA and Comex Good Delivery Lists are built. These lists are more than mere compilations of names; they are veritable seals of approval granted to mints and refineries that meet stringent standards of quality, transparency, and authenticity. When a producer's name graces these lists, it signifies more than a nod of recognition—it is an affirmation of their commitment to excellence, their dedication to crafting products that stand as paragons of integrity.

The LBMA Good Delivery List, akin to a hall of fame for precious metal producers, is a testament to the meticulous craftsmanship and ethical practices of the entities featured. Minted by the London Bullion Market Association, this list is an authoritative source that embodies trust, elevating the status of producers whose products meet the exacting requirements set forth by the LBMA. When you invest in products from mints or refineries listed here, you're essentially choosing a partner whose reputation aligns with the highest echelons of credibility.

The Comex Good Delivery List, crafted by the Commodity Exchange, carries echoes of assurance in the world of precious metal futures and options trading. Producers featured on this list have demonstrated their commitment to delivering products that meet the specifications outlined by the Comex. This commitment reverberates through the products they offer, imparting a sense of trust to potential buyers and ensuring a smooth flow of transactions within the dynamic Comex marketplace.

The relationship between the LBMA and Comex Good Delivery Lists and resale potential is akin to a golden thread weaving through precious metal investments' tapestry. Products from mints and refineries listed on these esteemed platforms carry an intrinsic mark of credibility—a stamp that reassures potential buyers of the product's authenticity and quality. This assurance translates to greater market acceptance and, consequently, higher resale potential, positioning you for a smoother, more profitable transition when the time comes to liquidate your investment.

In the cosmos of precious metal investments, where stars twinkle with the promise of value and authenticity, the LBMA and Comex Good Delivery Lists shine as guiding stars. Their presence adds an extra layer of assurance to your investment journey, ensuring your choices are anchored in credibility and market recognition. By aligning your investments with the producers featured on these reputable platforms, you're navigating the night sky with a celestial map—one that leads to a seamless investment experience, from acquisition to resale, and places your investment journey on a trajectory of authenticity and success.

4.4: THE COST OF CONFIDENCE: PREMIUMS AND ASSURANCE

In the tapestry of precious metal investments, the interplay between premiums and assurance weaves a story of value that transcends mere numbers. Investing in products from esteemed producers often entails paying a slightly higher premium upfront—a cost that, when seen through the lens of confidence, delivers a treasure trove of authenticity, quality, and future liquidity. As you delve into the nuances of this delicate balance between cost and confidence, you'll uncover a truth that goes beyond the initial investment—a truth that resonates deeply with the essence of a prudent investor's journey.

While numbers have their place in the world of investments, there are intangible factors that carry weight beyond mere digits. The premium associated with products from esteemed producers is not merely an added expense; it's an investment in assurance that the reputation, legacy, and trust of a respected brand back your investment. This assurance is invaluable; a cocoon of certainty envelops your investment, safeguarding it against doubts and uncertainties.

In pursuing investments that stand the test of time, peace of mind is a currency of immeasurable worth. The peace of mind from knowing your investment bears the mark of authenticity and quality is a priceless dividend that transcends the initial premium. This sense of security resonates through each ounce of metal you hold, casting a reassuring glow that strengthens your investment journey.

As an investor, the horizon extends beyond the initial acquisition to resale potential. Here, the economics of future value come into play. Products from reputable mints and refineries carry with them the potential to command a higher resale price down the line. The trust they inspire in potential buyers and their inherent quality positions them as coveted assets with a competitive edge. The premium you paid at the outset transforms into a cornerstone of future value, underscoring the wisdom of your investment choices.

Just as a symphony is composed of various instruments that blend harmoniously to create a masterpiece, the symphony of premiums and potential creates a melody of investment wisdom. The slightly higher premium you pay at the beginning harmonizes with the promise of authenticity, quality, and future liquidity. This harmony resonates through time, enriching your investment experience with a narrative of prudence, confidence, and foresight.

As you navigate the landscape of precious metal investments, remember that the cost of confidence transcends the mere numbers on an invoice. It's an investment in a narrative of authenticity, quality, and future value. The assurance that comes from investing in products from esteemed producers enriches your journey, casting a light on the path ahead. With each ounce of metal, you forge a connection not just to the preciousness of the metal itself but to the legacy of a respected brand—a connection that shapes your investment experience with clarity, assurance, and the promise of a prosperous future.

4.5: BUILDING A STRONG FOUNDATION

In the realm of precious metal investments, brand reputation, and resale value stand as pillars that support your journey toward financial security and growth. Choosing products from renowned producers sets a strong foundation for your portfolio, underpinned by authenticity, quality, and the promise of favorable resale opportunities. As you proceed on this investment odyssey, remember that every coin and bar from a respected mint or refinery carries not only the weight of precious metal but also the weight of trust and potential prosperity. Armed with this understanding, you're poised to navigate the intricate landscape of precious metal investments with confidence and foresight.

CHAPTER 5: VARIOUS SIZES OF GOLD AND SILVER PRODUCTS

In the world of precious metal investments, the diversity of options is a testament to the flexibility and inclusivity of the market. Gold and silver, two coveted metals, offer a range of sizes that cater to varying preferences and investment objectives. This chapter delves into the sizes available for gold and silver products, shedding light on the concept of premiums and how they intersect with different sizes and types of investments.

5.1: FROM MINUSCULE TO MIGHTY: THE SPECTRUM OF SIZES

In the grand tapestry of gold and silver investments, the spectrum of sizes weaves a rich narrative, each thread contributing to a story of versatility, accessibility, and value. As you unravel the intricacies of this spectrum, you'll discover that it encompasses a diverse array of sizes, each with its unique set of characteristics. From minuscule fractions to mighty bulk options, this spectrum reflects investors' diverse preferences and aspirations, painting a picture of a market that caters to every palette.

At one end of the spectrum lie the minuscule increments—fractional sizes that sparkle with charm and accessibility. One-gram gold coins and small silver bars, akin to delicate gems, cater to those who seek not only the allure of precious metals but also the convenience of divisibility. These tiny treasures are more than just investments; they are tokens of elegance, making them popular choices for gifting or trading. The beauty of these minuscule pieces lies not just in their metal content but in the stories they hold and the emotions they evoke.

The stalwarts occupy the heart of the spectrum—the one-ounce coins and bars that bridge the gap between convenience and value. These sizes strike a harmonious balance, offering a tangible presence while retaining the essence of investment-grade purity. Their popularity stems from their versatility; they are accessible to a wide range of investors, from novices embarking on their journey to seasoned individuals seeking to diversify their portfolios.

As you journey along the spectrum, you encounter the allure of bulk options—kilogram bars and industrial-sized thousand-ounce bars that beckon to investors with an appetite for greater quantities and lower premiums. These mighty options resonate with those who envision their investments in grandeur, who seek not just the gleam of metal but the weight of wealth. The ability to acquire a larger amount of precious metal content at a lower premium per ounce adds an extra layer of value to these options, appealing to those who see the investment potential in abundance.

The spectrum of sizes is not merely a linear progression; it's a realm of personalization and preference. A single size does not bind investors; they can choose the size that resonates with their goals, aspirations, and vision. The choice of size reflects an individual's investment philosophy—whether they prioritize convenience, divisibility, value, or sheer abundance. This personal touch adds depth to the investment experience, transforming it from a transaction into an expression of individuality.

In the symphony of gold and silver investments, the spectrum of sizes is the palette from which investors paint their financial masterpieces. Each size contributes to a symphony of diversity and possibility, from the delicate strokes of minuscule fractions to the bold splashes of bulk options. As you navigate this spectrum, remember that your choice of size reflects your unique vision—a vision that encompasses convenience, value, elegance, and abundance. By choosing the sizes that resonate with your aspirations, you're not just investing in precious metals; you're investing in the richness of your narrative—a narrative that blends seamlessly with the tapestry of the market, contributing to a story of individuality, value, and prosperity.

5.2: THE INTRICACIES OF PREMIUMS: UNVEILING THE DYNAMICS

Within precious metal investments, the term "premium" unfurls as a pivotal concept, a dynamic that influences the delicate balance between value and cost. While seemingly straightforward, the interplay of premiums reveals a tapestry of nuances that intertwines with size, type, and investor preferences, shaping the investment landscape in profound ways. As we step into this arena of premiums, we embark on a journey of discovery that exposes the intricate dance between value, cost, and individual aspirations.

At its core, the premium is a revelation of the difference between the spot price of the precious metal and the total cost of acquiring a specific product. It's a figure that carries weight far beyond its numerical value; it reflects the market's perception of worth, authenticity, and desirability. Unveiling the dynamics of premiums allows us to penetrate the surface of investments, delving into the layers that shape our decisions and inform our perceptions.

As we navigate the spectrum of sizes and types in precious metal investments, the premium emerges as a symphony conductor, orchestrating the harmony between value and investment goals. Smaller products, often adorned with higher premiums, extend an invitation to collectors and those who treasure divisibility. These miniature masterpieces evoke emotions beyond their metal content, appealing to the sentimental and aesthetic aspects of investment.

On the other side of the stage, larger products step forward, revealing their allure—lower premiums per ounce that cater to investors who place a premium on cost efficiency and the potential for bulk transactions. This dynamic equilibrium between premium and size/type underscores the investment experience's multifaceted nature, where each choice resonates with different motivations and preferences.

The dynamics of premiums pivot around investor motivations, spotlighting the diversity of aspirations that animate the precious metal landscape. Collectors, drawn to the stories and artistry behind the metal, find allure in higher premiums attached to smaller, intricate pieces. Investors seeking intrinsic value and potential returns assess larger pieces with lower premiums as a gateway to greater cost efficiency. Traders, maneuvering the ebb and flow of markets, navigate premiums as a transient landscape, seizing opportunities as they arise.

The tale of premiums extends beyond numbers—it's a narrative woven with threads of value, choice, and perception. The premium you pay is not just an additional cost; it's an investment in the product's character, legacy, and potential liquidity. It reflects the product's journey—from the mint to your hands and, potentially, back to the market. Recognizing this narrative enriches the investment experience, allowing you to view premiums not as a burden but as a passport to a world of authenticity, value, and potential.

As you navigate the intricate dance of premiums, remember that every ounce of precious metal carries a story that intertwines with yours. The premium, far from being a mere expense, is an investment in that narrative—a narrative that encapsulates value, aspiration, and trust. By understanding the dynamics of premiums, you unlock the soul of your investments, allowing them to resonate with your individual goals and dreams. The journey into premiums is the heart of investments—an exploration that reveals not just the numbers but the essence of value and meaning that underscores every piece of precious metal you hold.

5.3: Size, Premiums, and Value Propositions

In the symphony of precious metal investments, the harmonious interplay between size and premiums orchestrates a melody of value propositions, each note resonating with distinct advantages and aspirations. As we delve into the artistry of investment decisions, we find that size and premiums craft a canvas upon which your unique investment path unfolds—a path imbued with flexibility, accessibility, and potential returns.

At the forefront of this composition are fractional sizes, their allure heightened by the melody of higher premiums. While these smaller pieces command a premium that harmonizes with their intricate beauty, they are far more than adornments; they embody flexibility and charm. Fractional sizes are akin to a versatile currency, suitable for bartering, emergency transactions, or gifts that carry financial and emotional value. Their compact nature conceals a world of possibilities, making them not just investments but instruments of adaptability in a rapidly evolving financial landscape.

The one-ounce products stand in the composition's heart—a bridge between accessibility and value, a nexus where convenience and aspiration converge. These sizes epitomize the essence of investment-grade purity while offering a tangible presence that reflects the precious metal's worth. The interplay between premiums and the value of one-ounce products is a delicate dance that reflects the aspirations of those who seek to balance accessibility with the potential for growth.

As the melody crescendos, the stage welcomes larger sizes—products with lower premiums and an air of elegance accompanying abundance. These sizes captivate investors with the allure of substantial holdings, echoing the promise of capitalizing on market movements and long-term appreciation. While lower premiums per ounce add to their appeal, their potential for a grander investment narrative draws the spotlight.

As an investor, you wield the baton that guides this symphony of sizes and premiums. Like a composer's creation, your investment journey is a masterpiece crafted by your unique goals and aspirations. The composition unfolds as you align your investment choices with your personal value propositions.

Are you drawn to the allure of fractional sizes, valuing flexibility and adaptability? Or does the bridge of one-ounce products resonate with your need for accessibility and value? The elegance of abundance offered by larger sizes captures your vision of a substantial investment narrative.

In the grand theater of investments, size and premiums harmonize to create a melody that echoes your aspirations. By understanding the interplay between these elements, you make informed choices and compose an investment symphony that resonates with your values, goals, and dreams. As you step onto this stage of possibilities, remember that every note—the allure of flexibility, the bridge of accessibility, or the elegance of abundance—contributes to the masterpiece of your investment journey.

5.4: Balancing Act: The Weight of Size and Premiums

In the symphony of precious metal investments, the delicate dance between size and premiums orchestrates a harmonious balance that carries the weight of your investment strategy, liquidity considerations, and your relationship with premiums. This balance is not just a transactional decision; it reflects your aspirations, resonating with the unique cadence of your financial journey.

The decision to embrace a specific size within precious metals is a strategic choice—an ode to your investment strategy, a strategic aria that echoes your investment horizon, and risk tolerance. With their elevated premiums, smaller sizes offer a unique liquidity advantage, inviting you into a world of flexibility, where swift transactions and divisibility reign supreme. These sizes cater to the tacticians, those who value the agility of adapting to market changes or sudden financial demands.

On the other hand, larger sizes paint a canvas of grandeur—a canvas that speaks to the cost-conscious investor, the visionary who sees the potential in lowering the overall cost per ounce. These sizes are a testament to strategic patience, an acknowledgment that while premiums may be lower, the potential for substantial capitalization over the long haul is ripe for the picking. They resonate with those who approach the investment landscape with a panoramic view, valuing economies of scale and the elegance of abundant holdings.

The journey through this balancing act is a reflection of your unique aspirations. It's a navigation charted by your investment goals, personal preferences, and financial objectives. As you tread this path, you'll find that each step carries the weight of deliberate decision-making, underpinned by your understanding of market dynamics and the role premiums play in your investment narrative.

Much like a composer selecting the notes that harmonize to create a symphony, you craft your investment sonata—a composition that melds size, premiums, and strategy into a harmonious melody. Whether you're drawn to the agility of smaller sizes, the vision of larger sizes, or the sweet spot of middle-ground one-ounce products, your investment choices contribute to the masterpiece of your financial journey.

In the grand theater of investments, size, and premiums, perform a duet that carries the weight of your financial dreams. By embracing the balance between size and premiums, you breathe life into your investment symphony—a symphony that crescendos with your aspirations, echoing the chorus of your strategic choices and resonating with the harmony of your long-term goals. As you navigate this balancing act, remember that every investment decision is a note—a note that enriches your symphony, making it uniquely yours.

5.5: Empowering Decision-Making

The universe of sizes within gold and silver investments presents possibilities. The journey from minute fractions to substantial bars unveils a realm rich with diversity and potential. As you traverse this spectrum, remember that size and premiums are integral facets that shape the value and appeal of each product. With this understanding, you can make well-informed choices that harmonize with your investment aspirations. Whether you're drawn to the intricacies of smaller products, the efficiency of larger bars, or the equilibrium of one-ounce coins, the diversity of sizes is your canvas for constructing a portfolio that aligns with your financial vision.

Chapter 6: Premiums and Liquidity

In the realm of precious metal investments, understanding the dynamics of premiums and liquidity is akin to deciphering a language that unlocks the true value of your holdings. This chapter serves as a guide to unraveling the concept of premiums, dispelling the misconception surrounding the liquidity of bars versus coins, and empowering you to navigate the terrain of precious metals with clarity and confidence.

6.1: Demystifying Premiums: The Crucial Difference

In precious metal investments, a crucial element awaits your understanding—premiums. These subtle differentials hold the key to unraveling the intricacies of your investment choices. To navigate this landscape confidently, let's embark on a journey of demystification, revealing premiums' profound significance.

At its core, the premium is a beacon that shines light on the relationship between the spot price of the metal and the comprehensive cost of acquiring a specific precious metal product. This nuanced interplay encapsulates many factors, each contributing to the final sum separating spot price from total cost. Production costs, the artistry involved in craftsmanship, and the legacy of the producer all converge to shape the premium.

The premium is more than a mere numerical figure—it's an alchemical blend of craftsmanship, production precision, and the entity's reputation that brings the product to life. Each precious metal product carries with it a unique premium woven from the threads of its inception. As you explore your investment avenues, understanding this concept offers you a discerning eye to evaluate the value a particular premium brings to your investment journey.

To fathom the significance of premiums, you must first acquaint yourself with the spot price—a reference point in the ever-fluctuating world of precious metals. Armed with this understanding, you can then grasp the implications of premiums, transcending the surface value to comprehend the intricate layers of worth they encompass.

As you stand at the crossroads of investment decisions, the demystification of premiums empowers you to make informed choices. The premium acts as a guiding star, illuminating the potential return on investment, the caliber of craftsmanship, and the legacy of the producer. Armed with this knowledge, you can precisely gauge each product's value proposition, aligning your investments with your financial goals.

As you tread the path of precious metal investments, remember that each premium is a chapter in the story of your portfolio. By understanding and demystifying the role premiums play, you embark on a journey of enlightenment that empowers you to discern the true worth of each product beyond the surface. Just as a skilled artisan hones their craft, your comprehension of premiums refines your investment choices, unveiling the hidden dimensions that contribute to the value of each precious metal piece.

6.2: Dispelling the Myth: Liquidity of Bars vs. Coins

In the labyrinthine world of precious metals, a prevailing myth holds sway—that coins monopolize liquidity, leaving bars in the shadows. However, let's embark on a journey of enlightenment to dispel this misconception and shed light on the liquidity equilibrium between coins and bars.

Coins have garnered their reputation as liquid assets due to their historical allure, artistic charm, and potential collectible value. Yet, it's time to unveil a truth often obscured—the liquidity of bars stands as a formidable counterpart. The misconception lies in viewing coins and bars through a myopic lens, neglecting the thriving ecosystem of reputable dealers who actively facilitate transactions for both forms.

The crux of liquidity transcends the physical form of investment—it hinges on the reputation of the product and the integrity of the dealers orchestrating the exchanges. Reputable precious metal dealers, recognized and trusted within the industry, play a pivotal role in the liquidity equation. These dealers seamlessly navigate the currents of both coins and bars, providing investors a platform to transform their holdings into liquid assets.

Like a river's flow, liquidity derives its strength from multiple tributaries. The lesson here is that the liquidity of your investment is not determined solely by its form but by the product's reputation and the dealer's competence. As you tread the path of precious metal investments, trust established dealers and products from esteemed mints or refineries. This art of decision-making ensures that liquidity is readily attainable whether your investment takes the form of coins or bars.

In precious metals, liquidity emerges as a fluid reality, not tethered to the confines of coins or bars. It's a testament to the integrity of reputable dealers and the worthiness of the products they facilitate. As the curtain falls on the myth, the truth shines—a well-informed investor, armed with knowledge and the guidance of respected dealers, can effortlessly navigate the seas of liquidity, whether they set sail with coins or navigate the currents with bars. The choice is yours, and the liquidity awaits.

6.3: REPUTABLE DEALERS: THE BRIDGE TO LIQUIDITY

In the intricate tapestry of the precious metals market, reputable dealers stand as the guardians of liquidity, wielding ethical practices and market expertise to bridge the gap between investment and transformation. These stalwarts serve as the indispensable conduits through which investors traverse the realm of buying and selling, ensuring a seamless journey from acquisition to liquidity.

At the heart of reputable dealers lies an unwavering commitment to ethical practices. Their integrity is a cornerstone of the trust investors place in them. These dealers conduct their transactions transparently, ensuring investors are empowered with the knowledge they need to make informed decisions. The ethical nexus extends to fair pricing, equitable dealings, and an unyielding dedication to providing value.

Reputable dealers are more than mere intermediaries; they are seasoned navigators of the intricate landscape of precious metal transactions. Whether you seek to acquire coins or bars, these dealers streamline the process, making it accessible, comprehensible, and swift. Their expertise guides you through the nuances, demystifying the complexities and ensuring your investment journey is marked by confidence.

In your quest for liquidity, a touchstone of distinction exists—the LBMA Good Delivery List and the Comex Good Delivery List. These revered directories showcase the entities that have attained the pinnacle of quality standards within the industry. By aligning yourself with dealers featured on these lists, you forge a connection to a network of trust, where liquidity is not a distant promise but a tangible reality.

Reputable dealers are not mere gatekeepers but catalysts for transforming investments into liquid assets. Their commitment to ethical practices, market acumen, and transparent dealings ensures that your precious metal holdings are poised for fluidity when the time comes. As you traverse the intricate landscape of precious metal investments, remember that your dealer choice is more than a transaction—it's the embodiment of your trust, the assurance of liquidity, and the cornerstone of a successful investment journey.

6.4: THE RESALE ADVANTAGE: TRUSTED BRAND IMPACT

In the intricate dance of precious metal investments, a decisive advantage emerges—the resonance of renowned brands in the resale arena. As an investor, aligning your portfolio with products from esteemed mints and refineries bestows upon you the coveted resale advantage—a seamless process that rests on the shoulders of trusted brand impact.

Established mints and refineries have cultivated a currency that transcends the metallic realm—confidence. This currency is forged through decades of commitment to quality, authenticity, and craftsmanship. When it comes time to part ways with your precious metal holdings, this trust dividend becomes your greatest asset, influencing the entire resale journey.

Investing in products from renowned producers is akin to holding a key that unlocks a world of immediate recognition. Potential buyers, individuals, collectors, or institutions, readily acknowledge the pedigree of established mints and refineries. The halo of trust enveloping these brands translates into an instant rapport, leading to quicker decisions and smoother negotiations.

As potential buyers clamor for products from reputable sources, your investments enjoy a competitive edge. The trust factor associated with established brands fuels demand, allowing you to command offers that reflect the true worth of your holdings. This competitive environment ensures that you are well-compensated for your investment and empowered to make informed decisions in the resale process.

In the realm of investments, time often plays a pivotal role. The resale advantage granted by the trusted brand impact is synonymous with speed. The recognition and confidence imbued by renowned producers expedite the transaction process. Quicker negotiations, agreements, and settlements are the hallmarks of this advantage, allowing you to capitalize on market conditions and make timely decisions.

In the grand tapestry of investments, the legacy of trust echoes louder than ever. The resonance of established mints and refineries transcends aesthetics and craftsmanship—it is a testament to a legacy meticulously crafted over time. As you navigate the seas of precious metal investments, remember that your decisions ripple into the future. Embrace the resale advantage offered by trusted brand impact, and let the trust dividend serve as the bedrock of your investment success.

6.5: Empowering Your Investment Journey

Understanding premiums and liquidity arm you with a dual-edged sword of knowledge as you navigate the precious metals landscape. By discerning the nuances of premiums, you can assess the intrinsic value of your investments and make well-informed decisions. Dispelling the liquidity myth liberates you from preconceived notions, allowing you to explore coins and bars with equal anticipation. As you journey forward, remember that your investment's liquidity is not solely tied to its form but is, in fact, intertwined with the product's reputation and the dealer's integrity. Equipped with this understanding, you're primed to navigate the realm of premiums and liquidity with unwavering confidence and insight.

CHAPTER 7: CONCLUSION AND RECAP

As we draw the curtains on exploring the world of precious metal investments, it's fitting to reflect on the key takeaways illuminating our journey. Through the intricate landscape of coins and bars, brand reputation and premiums, sizes, and liquidity, we've navigated the diverse facets that shape the decisions of every savvy investor. Let's recap the insights that now serve as the foundation of your understanding.

7.1: A JOURNEY OF DISCOVERY

Our journey began by acknowledging the allure of precious metals as tangible assets that transcend time, history, and cultural significance. The potential of gold and silver to act as a hedge against economic uncertainties and diversify portfolios laid the groundwork for our exploration.

7.2: COMMON THREADS IN COINS AND BARS

We unveiled the standard features that bind coins and bars, such as manufacturer information, weight, purity, and type of metal. These shared attributes in every piece of precious metal serve as the bedrock of authenticity and value.

7.3: Reputation and Resale Value

The role of reputable producers emerged as a pivotal factor in your investment journey. We emphasized the relationship between brand reputation and resale value, showcasing how products from trusted sources enjoy greater liquidity and command higher resale prices.

7.4: Size, Premiums, and Liquidity

Diving into the sizes available for gold and silver products, we demystified the concept of premiums—the difference between spot price and total cost. We dispelled that bars are less liquid than coins, underscoring that both can be easily sold through reputable dealers.

7.5: Equipped for Success

Our journey reaches its culmination with a profound appreciation for the intricacies of precious metal investments. With knowledge about coins and bars, brand reputation, premiums, sizes, and liquidity, you're primed to make strategic investment decisions that align with your financial aspirations.

7.6: An Ongoing Adventure

As you navigate the intricate world of precious metal investments, remember that every decision you make should be rooted in a thorough understanding of the nuances at play. The journey is ongoing, and as markets evolve and circumstances change, your knowledge will be your most valuable asset.

7.7: Unveiling a Golden Opportunity

Before embarking on any investment endeavor, the final message to engrave in your mind is the importance of understanding the differences between coins and bars. Armed with this knowledge, you possess the tools to make informed decisions that will shape your investment portfolio for years to come.

7.8: To the Future

As you tread the path of precious metal investments, may your journey be marked by wisdom, success, and a continued passion for uncovering the hidden treasures within the realm of gold and silver. Your grasp of the intricacies has the potential to unveil a golden opportunity that stands the test of time.

With this, we conclude our exploration, wishing you prosperity and fulfillment in your precious metal investment endeavors.

CONCLUSION

Coin collecting is a time-consuming hobby. So, be patient and pay attention to the quality. Coin collectors have the opportunity to learn a lot about history, metal, and other topics. It's a fantastic moment to be a numismatist right now. You can also show your kids how to collect coins and save them. It offers you pleasure. It may occasionally be a pleasant surprise or an unexpected offer. People collect coins for a variety of reasons. Many people are enthralled by the journey that any penny has taken, traveling through the hands and lives of many people who lived decades, if not centuries ago. It's possible that anyone, even celebrities, and historical figures, came into contact with the coins. Someone who can take you on a virtual tour of a country's historical path.

It's possible that someone else may be enthralled by the idea of collecting something that is both common and valuable, perhaps in a way that few people are aware of. They enjoy being the ones who are privy to these secrets that are buried in plain sight. For others, it may just be a pleasurable and thrilling pastime that also serves as a short or long-term investment. A treasure that you may build up little by little, day by day, with little significant outlay at first, and eventually end up with a valuable collection worth far more than the individual bits you accumulated along the way.

Whatever your reason or motive, whether it's one of the aforementioned or something more personal and unique. This book has assisted you in finding a means to begin and some guidance in taking your first steps boldly into this beautiful adventure. In this book, you will learn the types and anatomy of a coin. Then, of course, this is only the beginning of a new interest for you.

Made in United States
Troutdale, OR
11/14/2023

14569279R00106